Drago Kunej, Urša Šivic (Eds.)

Trapped in Folklore?

AF720828

Musikethnologie
Ethnomusicology

Band / Volume 7

LIT

Trapped in Folklore?

Studies in Music and Dance Tradition and Their Contemporary Transformations

edited by

Drago Kunej and Urša Šivic

LIT

Cover image: Participants of a bagpipe camp. Kaposvár, 1982.
Photo: unknown photographer.

Financially supported by Glasbenonarodopisni inštitut ZRC SAZU, Ljubljana, Slovenia.

Layout: Natalija Stanivuk.

Bibliographic information published by the Deutsche Nationalbibliothek
The Deutsche Nationalbibliothek lists this publication in the Deutsche Nationalbibliografie; detailed bibliographic data are available in the Internet at http://dnb.d-nb.de.

ISBN 978-3-643-90232-0

A catalogue record for this book is available from the British Library

©LIT VERLAG GmbH & Co. KG Wien,
Zweigniederlassung Zürich 2013
Klosbachstr. 107
CH-8032 Zürich
Tel. +41 (0) 44-251 75 05
Fax +41 (0) 44-251 75 06
E-Mail: zuerich@lit-verlag.ch
http://www.lit-verlag.ch

LIT VERLAG Dr. W. Hopf
Berlin 2013
Fresnostr. 2
D-48159 Münster
Tel. +49 (0) 2 51-62 03 20
Fax +49 (0) 2 51-23 19 72
E-Mail: lit@lit-verlag.de
http://www.lit-verlag.de

Distribution:
In Germany: LIT Verlag Fresnostr. 2, D-48159 Münster
Tel. +49 (0) 2 51-620 32 22, Fax +49 (0) 2 51-922 60 99, E-mail: vertrieb@lit-verlag.de

In Austria: Medienlogistik Pichler-ÖBZ, e-mail: mlo@medien-logistik.at
In Switzerland: B + M Buch- und Medienvertrieb, e-mail: order@buch-medien.ch
In the UK: Global Book Marketing, e-mail: mo@centralbooks.com
In North America: International Specialized Book Services, e-mail: orders@isbs.com
e-books are available at www.litwebshop.de

CONTENTS

Drago Kunej and Urša Šivic

FOLK MUSIC TRAPPED IN FOLKLORE?

This thematic publication is rather provocatively entitled *Trapped in Folklore?* Our goals were to create a common denominator connecting the articles of different authors, and to determine whether a certain musical phenomenon can be trapped in tradition and folklore or not. The question mark in the chosen title implies that the thought "trapped in folklore" is not a thesis but a hypothesis, or a continuous and essential scholarly query regarding the place, the role and the meaning of the phenomenon discussed. Included are questions as to whether the selected musical phenomenon are a fossilised form of tradition, folklore and folklorism and, as such, are trapped in a museum-like image isolated from contemporary cultural life, or whether we are looking at active events, changes and adjustments within contemporary society.

The publication consists of a selection of articles presented by scholars from different countries and backgrounds at the international interdisciplinary symposium *What to Do with Folklore?*, an event held in Ljubljana in 2009 and organised by the Institute of Ethnomusicology at the Scientific Research Centre of the Slovenian Academy of Sciences and Arts in order to mark its 75th anniversary. The symposium hosted numerous researchers from the fields of folkloristics, ethnomusicology, ethnology, anthropology, Slavic studies, musicology, sociology and other areas of expertise, who came together to present their thoughts on folklore as the broadest of folk spiritual cultures, and on the entwining of folklore's traditions and heritage with its contemporary transformations. The symposium's title was not a coincidence. In fact it was taken from the title of an article written in 1975 by Zmaga Kumer (1924–2008), a renowned Slovenian ethnomusicologist and expert on musical heritage, who was a long-time associate of the Institute. The symposium commemorated her memory.

The common denominator of the articles presented, which were written specifically for this publication, is folk music and those folklore phenomenon closely connected to it. Consequently the articles' thematic derives mostly from the fields of ethnomusicology and ethnochoreology, and from research into the documentation and usage of archival material on folk music. The authors' views on folk music vary as some of them discuss folk music within the narrowest meaning of the term, while others take a broader approach and discuss it in connection with its contemporary manifestations. For example, folk music is discussed by Zoltan Szabó and Katalin Juhász who present bagpipes, the Hungarian folk instrument, and bagpipe music in the historical context of a revival movement. David Verbuč discusses folklore texts in music performances and music performance events set up by the inhabitants of a specific geographical location (the village of Primož near Ljubno in Slovenia) as well as the functions of these performances, their spatial aspects, and how cultural values and meanings were reflected and generated through them. Urša Šivic discusses traditional Balkan brass band music as a form transplanted into another cultural and geographical space.

Most of the authors though, tend to move away from discussing folk music in the narrowest meaning of the term. They often link it to other music types or they deal with newer music practices and manifestations. Liz Mellish and Nick Green present traditional folk dance performance in the 21st century through the comparison of two folk dances from different geographic and political environments. Alma Bejtullahu looks at Slovenian and Kosovar folk music in terms of contemporary popular music styles, while Selena Rakočević discusses music as an integral part of contemporary female customs. Zlata Marjanović follows a selected song throughout a longer historical context and in a broader geographical space (Slovenia, Croatia, Serbia, Montenegro) and further discusses its various genres, social contexts and meanings.

Three of the authors chose recorded folk music, an often used resource for scientific research, as their discussion background. And so Rebeka Kunej analyses old gramophone records and their content as a scientific resource in ethnochoreological research in Slovenia. Similarly, Drago Kunej discusses the advantages and disadvantages of recorded folk audio material as an audio resource for users and researchers in various disciplines, while Susanne Ziegler stresses the importance of historical recordings of folk music in the research of music worldwide and points out that these recordings are often trapped in archives and not open to public access.

Although the authors in their articles, which are methodologically varied, deal with different musical and musical-folkloristic phenomenon, the answers to the main question of entrapment in folklore present a more or less unified picture. The analyses show an openness to the concept of space of folklore or music, in which the authors understand the (non-)entrapment in folklore in different ways.

For some this is a folklorised phenomenon in modern times, while others see it as a folklore phenomenon that has seen a transformation in the present. For example, the topic of the article by Szabó and Juhász, which deals with the reconstruction and revival of past traditions in bagpipe making and usage, is in fact clear folklorisation. Despite the fact that the activities described are derived from fossilized, "museified" folklore, the authors defend non-entrapment in folklore with the following argument: "We are not trapped in a 'fossilized' tradition that lost its function a long time ago, we are open to novelties and we provide free passage between the authentic (old, traditional, nowadays hardly alive) folklore and the men of today (modern culture)." Similarly, Mellish and Green conclude in their article that two specific traditions, Romanian *căluş* and English morris, have continued to be practiced as living traditions and so have not become "trapped in folklore" in a form that resisted change. This is not just represented by a few villages where these traditions still exist within their communities, but by a wider organisation of dance groups that continue to perform these traditions in their respective countries in the 21st century; the revivalist morris teams of England and the folk ensembles of Romania. The contribution by Rakočević, which focuses on women in the context of personal and social expression, also examines the custom of ritual act in present times. Although we are dealing with the revival of a custom, today it presents an "inverted reproduction of the repressive everyday reality of women, not only at the level of the rural social community, but also within the complex family and matrimonial relations in this area." The author concludes that folklorism, while seemingly pure, has a rather more complex social context, "*Revena* custom still functions not as an archaism, a museum artefact, but rather as an important emotional release from oppressive hierarchical conditions and as a potential corrective to outdated social relations at the local level." Ultimately it is the insight into the context of this custom demonstrates that women's behaviour functions free of folklore in order "to feel free and behave freely without oppressive social restrictions."

Other authors shed light on (non-)entrapment in folklore by comparing the traditional and the new within the framework of the creative process. Although some deal with a revived form of tradition, they conclude that tradition and its revival is not always binding. So, two authors Szabó and Juhász compare the learning and preservation of tradition with language, "Once learning this 'language' anyone can express themselves freely. Moreover he/she may mix it with other 'languages,' too. Thus, the combination of tradition and creativity results in a large spectrum within both instrument manufacturing and music itself." The creativity mentioned by these authors is also used by Šivic to debate the question in the title "trapped in folklore." On the one hand she recognises entrapment within the researched musical activities in the sense of "its music characteristics, political and historical ties." On the other hand it is creativity which should prove that we are not dealing with entrapment in folklore but with "adaptations that are free and not trapped in folklore in the sense of music creativity." Marjanović describes the way a selected song travelled through a specific historical period and geographical space and recognises the porous quality of folklore by admitting that this song has its own contextual place in each period and geographical space as "each nation has accepted the Tune as 'their own' and because each nation is identified through the Tune." Bejtullahu, on the other hand, looks at tradition in present times from a different perspective. Her article discusses women musicians and the instruments and music they play. The author observes her selected topic in two "research areas—Kosovo and Slovenia—as two completely separate areas" and through a comparison of the past and present in the context of the modernisation of society and the general as well as musical, emancipation and professionalization of women. Researching the case of two all-female ensembles she comes to the conclusion that "in the case of *çifteli* ensembles in Kosovo, the strictly traditional orientation of the repertoire caused women to reach out mostly to the rural public sphere and only later, with the loosening of this norm, were they able to keep up with their listenership. On the other hand the tamboura ensembles that emerged as a new and more universal practice, have achieved an interesting and almost eternal status among Slovenian musicians." She notes that "the way women negotiate and reposition themselves as musicians is an interesting example of how women either work within the proverbial 'entrapment of folklore' or follow the completely opposite path."

Unlike the articles mentioned so far, some authors view entrapment in folklore as a stereotypical and limited way to research and document of folklore music phenomenon and accompanying scholarly thought. Rebeka Kunej, for example, uses the analysis of gramophone records to point out that "in order to control the subject of interest researchers have divided the definition of folklore into genres, categories and other definitions and breakdowns. This is to help us define different performance practices, their features of style and products. However, we forget that the boundaries of folklore can be very fluid and difficult to define, changeable and inconclusive, as can our definitions. By cementing these boundaries we can become trapped in folklore, always looking only at the folk music and folk dance, and forgetting to look over the picket fence to the neighbours called popular, mass or commercial music." Similarly Drago Kunej concludes that ethnomusicology and folklore studies often consider sound recordings an almost perfect scholarly resource for studying folk music, even though this belief is fairly naive and lacks any real theoretical bases. Researchers are therefore too frequently trapped in an insufficiently critical mode of using sound recordings and tend to trust them too blindly as reliable scholarly resources when conducting research in ethnomusicology and folklore studies. Verbuč, who follows folklore texts in a fairly narrow geographical and temporal space (i.e. performance events in Primož, Slovenia; their structure, function, and meaning, and their contextualization and re-contextualization of folklore texts), also comes to similar conclusions: "Traditional life and folk music among Primož' villagers existed at the beginning of the 2000s in a transformed form, as modifications of their older cultural and social practices." Institutions, scholars, and cultural workers—at a national, regional, and local level—"stimulate, promote, and organize staged folklore and tourist representations of past folklore 'texts,' customs, songs and tunes, and thus impose their comprehension of past traditions on many participants who, often then subsequently 'trapped by folklore,' live and traverse between their vital community traditions on one side and condensed and manufactured traditions on the other." Finally, as an example of a particular entrapment in folklore, Ziegler uses her own experience with archival collection of wax cylinders in the Berlin Phonogramm-Archiv to conclude that such historical collections form a special genre among the holdings of ethnomusicological archives; they are unique historical sources, but also cause different kinds of problems. She also points out that historical recordings need special treatment, not only because of their fragile and sensitive physical material, but also because of their unique content. But if we cannot gain information from historical examples of music cultures, and without background information, "these recordings would be trapped in the archive, and at the same time trapped in history; they cannot be used for ethnomusicological research."

Questions like "What to do with folklore?" and the related "Trapped in folklore?" open up many possibilities for reflection and prompt different answers. Views on tradition and folklore differ and change and transform with time just as tradition and folklore change and transform by themselves. The question Zmaga Kumer posed in 1975 in her booklet *What to Do with Folklore?* was at the time considered to be the focal point in folkloristics: how to stop, or at least curb, the process of forgetting tradition, and how to contribute to the understanding of folklore. Present views on folklore are often different and also differ from each other. The lay public tends to look back in the past and its views resemble those "criticised" by Zmaga Kumer in her 1975 work. The prevailing view in the field of folkloristics at present is more open and "understanding" of various forms of folklore phenomenon, which is understandable as openness and acceptability are typical of present global cultural trends, hybridism and "otherness," along with new forms and new meanings. The aim of this publication entitled *Trapped in Folklore?* is to present the modernity, openness and diversity of views on folklore and to create a connection between (past and present) folklore phenomenon, between researchers and between their fields of expertise.

Zoltán Szabó and Katalin Juhász

BAGPIPE REVIVAL IN HUNGARY: *TÁNCHÁZ* MODEL AS PRACTICE AND TRANSMISSION OF TRADITION

ABSTRACT

The essence of the Hungarian folk music and dance revival movement that started in the 1970s was the acquisition of authentic folklore as a "mother tongue." The discovery of the bagpipe and the popularity of the bagpipe music was part of this movement. This study intends to introduce some typical activities of the Hungarian bagpipe revival including ways of obtaining knowledge, research, and bagpipe manufacture. It is a part of a wider research based primarily on the authors' personal experiences, on interviews conducted with instrument players and some relevant professional sources.

Key words: bagpipe revival, Hungary, *táncház* model, dance house

INTRODUCTION

The well known special Hungarian *táncház* (dance-house) model[1] of teaching folk dance and music combines traditional forms of acquisition with modern pedagogical and academic methods. Participants acquire knowledge from experienced members or tradition bearers by direct observation and imitation, while using their own individual level of creativity to develop their competence and ability. This is complemented by handicraft activities and ethnographic presentations. Anyone regardless of age, competence or prior exposure can become an active participant. The aim is to establish a value-based, community building, entertaining yet educational form of recreational activity through the practice and transmission of intangible cultural heritage. *Táncház* method is also utilized in art schools and

1 This model for the transmission of intangible cultural heritage was selected for the Register of Best Safeguarding Practices by UNESCO Intergovernmental Committee for the Safeguarding of Intangible Heritage in 2011.

all levels of education, and influences folk dance and music performance. The *táncház* movement can be very well-defined in space and in time, bringing along revolutionary changes in the stage performance, as well as generating a specifically complex subculture with its own professional and "social" structure (Juhász 1993), life style and tastes. The emerging folk culture revival movement[2] in the 1970s witnessed a new development in Hungarian bagpipe (*duda*) culture, too. That time, a number of key figures of that movement were intent on resurrecting the instrument. They began studying extant literature and talking to surviving pipers in an attempt to relearn the techniques involved in bagpipe craftsmanship and performance.

Pipers have always been in a special, quite often marginal position within society. They stood out from the others by their special knowledge that is essential for playing the bagpipe and which was often considered as coming from the devil itself. Naturally this "satanic" origin is never mentioned nowadays, but we can say that the new generation of pipers emerging from the dance house movement is also fundamentally different from players of other, more classical instruments. The bagpipe is an instrument that is made using a special handicraft technique and it needs constant maintenance and alterations, which requires the player not only to possess musical talent and playing techniques but also remarkable instrument-building "craftsman's" skills.

The study investigates the way that the complex knowledge which forms the background of the traditional bagpipe music and manufacturing the instrument gets to the representatives of the folk revival and public nowadays. On the other hand we explore the activities, roles and functions in which the new generations of Hungarian bagpipers are involved.

In our analysis we follow the model of Lundberg, Malm and Ronström to differentiate the large group of bagpipers. We classify the actors of a music culture in three categories (i.e. "doers," "knowers" and "makers")

2 The latest survey in English to date see Balogh and Fülemile 2008 in a thematic issue of the journal *Hungarian Studies* 22 (2008): 1–2.

according to their roles and their relationship to the given music culture.[3] Our analysis is based primarily on the authors' personal experiences, on interviews[4] conducted with instrument players and some relevant professional sources.

We study the three categories of actors and activities mentioned focusing on the Hungarian bagpipe revival. Different forms of knowledge acquisition such as amateur fieldwork, self-education and institutional education are presented in the paper. We also pay attention to the special methodology and auxiliary materials used in the education. The professionalization of the bagpipers from revival fan to ethnomusicologist will be discussed, too. The emergence and the development of the bagpipe manufacture gets a separate chapter, where we present the influence of the needs of the stage on the innovations.

OBTAINING KNOWLEDGE

Discovering Bagpipe – Meeting Traditional Pipers

One of the main characteristics of the dance house movement is that it originates in the city, far from the rural world and the folk tradition. It is urban people who get involved in rural music and folk dances, finding in it a special, "exotic" experience,[5] not unlike meeting the culture of distant peoples. Although in the early 1970s there were shepherd pipers alive in Hungary, it was typical for the future revival pipers to glimpse their first instrument abroad (e.g. Sándor Csoóri Jr. and István Berán in Bulgaria,

3 Lundberg et al. 2003: 50–52, see also Lundberg 2007. For a more detailed description of this study see Juhász 2010.

4 Most of the interviews were conducted between 1995 and 2004. The collection of data is continuous, as we conduct additional fieldwork.

5 Beside exoticism, there has naturally been in Hungary the motive of national feeling that had successfully broken the silence around the Hungarian minorities living in the neighbouring countries, and meant a symbolic opposition against the existing "socialist" regime. This question has been discussed in detail by many Hungarian analyzers of the dance house movement; see for instance, Balogh and Fülemüle 2008, Kiss 2006.

Fig. 1: Sándor Csoóri and András Seres, beginning of 1980s. Photo: unknown photographer.

Béla Ágoston in Italy). As Ferenc Tobak said: "I first saw a bagpipe at the Windmill Restaurant in Sozopol, Bulgaria in 1979. A piper was playing there, accompanied by a drum. The next year I bought my own first bagpipe, a *gaida*, at a news-stand in Sophia, though it turned out later that the instrument was not really usable. The same summer I made my first Hungarian bagpipe chanter, using the dimensions I had observed on the Bulgarian instrument."[6]

In the 1960s János Manga could find as many as sixteen traditional pipers, but only two of them had their bagpipes bound, in usable condition. The Budapest musicians setting out for the former Upper Hungary in the first years of the dance house movement could still find four or five performers. It was extremely important for them to meet traditional pipers in person, as the chief "methodical" trick of the dance house movement lay in learning directly from the performers. During the mid-1970s, Csoóri tracked down two Palóc pipers, who could not only teach him the basics of

6 Ferenc Tobak, personal communication with Katalin Juhász, August 2002.

the instrument and supply him with parts, but could also provide a considerable amount of specialised knowledge that was not obtainable from sheet music or recordings. As Csoóri tells it, when the Ipolypalást piper János Szikora parted with his instrument, he literally bid it farewell, saying "'Good-bye pipe! We've suffered much together!' Then he went out from the room, leaving me there with the bagpipe" (Bankó 1994: 179).

Of his own learning process, József Kozák recounted: "I first heard a recording of real Hungarian bagpipe music in the mid-1970s. It was that performance by the head shepherd from Borsosberény, József Kós, that made me want above all else to master this instrument. As it turned out, perusing available folk music and ethnographic sources wasn't enough. I needed to find living, performing pipers, either at home or in neighbouring countries. I visited corners of the Carpathian Basin where the Hungarian *duda* or some other double-chanter bagpipe could still be found. I learned the nitty-gritty of bagpipe manufacture, a feat no more difficult than learning to play the instrument itself" (Szabó 2004: 58).

In the 1970s and 80s Sándor Csoóri Jr. and his pupils also strived, almost moving from village to village, to find the remaining representatives of the shepherd piper-flutist tradition. They looked around in Nógrád county and its surroundings especially, where the piper tradition could survive the longest. Unfortunately Ernő Kukucska, the last known piper in Nógrád at the time, had not been willing to play the instrument: "Despite all their efforts, the piper generation of the dance houses had to make do with studying his recordings, because whenever they asked him to play the bagpipe, he would tell them the same, 'I no longer care for making music, I don't play, I don't go, don't ask me'" (Juhász 1994: 3). It was eventually in 1993 that Zoltán Juhász and his collector-friends could make film and tape recordings with Ernő Kukucska. From these, one can learn such peculiarities of technique as would be impossible to catch merely by the ear (Juhász 1994: 3).

In the 1990s, the "rediscovery" of Tereske shepherd István Pál (1919) brought significant change to the world of Hungarian bagpipe music.

Fig. 2: István Pál, the last Hungarian traditional bagpiper and Zoltán Juhász. Budapest, 2007. Photo: Béla Kása.

János Manga had photographed the young shepherd/piper in 1936,[7] after which he had played less and less frequently, until finally, in the 1970s, his wife had sold his bagpipe. It was to the credit of Gergely Agócs and Zoltán Juhász that after they had found the elderly Pál in 1992, he picked up an instrument again in 1993, and since then, an entire series of scientific publications and audio recordings on the legacy of "the last piper" have been produced.[8]

István Pál performs regularly with his young followers, but he also makes instruments (bagpipes, flutes) and, with the assistance of professional folk music teachers, he imparts his vocal and instrumental skills to those wishing to learn at folk music courses and camps.

7 The photo may be found in the Palóc Museum in Balassagyarmat: F.680.

8 See f.e.: Juhász Z. 1998.

Despite Pál's fame as the "last piper," Hungary boasts a second surviving piper/instrument maker from the tiny Croatian Dráva River community of Tótújfalu in Baranya County. The elderly Croatian piper Pál Gadányi (1932) owes his "discovery" to the Baranya Dance Ensemble, Vujicsics, and Vizin bands (their repertoire is based on the traditional music and dance of South Slavic minorities living in Hungary), who began inviting him to play at their performances.[9] Gadányi also performs with two village singers in shows organised as part of the amateur folk music movement. In his own village he plays only in pubs and at church processions, while neighbouring villages invite him to play at local fairs, as the elderly still enjoy hearing the bagpipe.

Archive Recordings as the Main Instruments of Learning

However much some would have it, neither traditional peasant culture, nor its component, music culture, can be sustained forever. It can only be fixed in the freeze-frame of its momentary state, as collectors' sound and film recordings literally "preserve" the music of the one-time bagpipe players. These recordings may now be the chief instruments of acquiring stylish and traditional bagpipe playing. If they cannot substitute for the experience of personal contacts, the recordings and their meticulously exact transcription into musical notation[10] can help the learner to reproduce the original sounding as accurately as possible. This scrupulous imitation is the first step in the process of learning. After acquiring the right amount of tunes with this method, the player, already possessing the style pertaining to the given region, becomes able after a while to perform tunes appropriately even from vocal recordings or sheet music.

The recordings made by professional ethnomusicologists and stored in archives (Juhász and Szabó 2010: 203–205) were not easily accessible for

9 Together with director János Tari, in 2004 Zoltán Szabó made a documentary about Pál Gadányi's activity as a bagpipe maker, called *The Gift of Fairies*.

10 The technique of transcribing folk music recordings had been brought to perfection by Béla Bartók and Zoltán Kodály. Their pupils and present-day followers employ the same method, listening several times to the slowed down recording, putting down the tiniest ornaments in musical notation.

the young pioneer pipers of the 1970s. If through an "insider" they could get hold of a recording from the Institute for Musicology at the Hungarian Academy of Sciences, or from the Museum of Ethnography, they passed it around as some gem and copied it to tape among friends. Pipers also tried to record the music of as many living pipers as possible, and these tapes were swapped and copied alike. With the folk music revival becoming widespread and institutionalized, with new digital devices and the internet, there are now several opportunities to access archive recordings. It is the former Institute of Education that deserves the credit for starting the publication of essential educational reference materials provided with sheet music and audio supplement (Juhász 1994, 1998). In 1981, within the frame of the Institute of Education, the "Professional House" was established and for two decades it served almost uniquely in Europe as an archive for video and audio recordings that could be visited freely by anyone, and where you could buy a cheap copy of any material. Nor could visitors be dissuaded by the poor conditions and out-of-date equipment owing to lack of funds; everyone took pleasure in browsing, and even amateur collectors placed their material, knowing that it would be in proper hands.

After 1990, similar workshops were established in the country, and pipers learnt about recordings preserved in country museums (Kaposvár, Pécs, Mohács, Győr). Another important step in this process was when some of them obtained a degree in ethnography since as museologists, they had "official" access to the often forgotten or neglected audio recordings and, through ever widening channels, could make them available for the public (Tanai 1995, Szabó 1991, 2001a, 2001b). Naturally they used these recordings for widening their own repertoires, as well as using them as educational materials.

Since the 1980s, the Folk Music Archive of the Institute for Musicology at the Academy of Sciences has published its series of archive recordings (Sárosi 1980, 1998; and the *Magyar Népzenei Antológia I–VII*), first on LPs, then on cassettes and finally on CDs, all of which the musicians were glad to receive. In recent decades an increasing number of archive materials have been brought out by (often private) publishers specializing in folk music, a great amount being bagpipe music (Lányi 2001, Stuber 2002). Besides the recordings listed above we must definitely mention the home-copied cassette and CD material used in the annual camps of "Egyszólam" band, comprising several hours' of recordings by bagpiper István Pál over 18 years.

For its 2004 exhibition, the Museum of Ethnography published a CD offering a taste of the Folk Music Collections' archive material. The editors intended to give a sample of each collector's compilation as well as of each great pipers' playing, considering it important to represent all types of the bagpipe used in the Carpathian Basin (Szabó and Pálóczy 2004).

Digitization has meant a new phase in the distribution of recordings, through which the archive material preserved in the Hungarian Heritage House (established in 2001 and comprising the former Professional House)[11], in the Institute for Musicology[12] and the Museum of Ethnography[13] has become accessible on the internet and, in part, is freely downloadable. What is more, the internet has helped to widen the scope, as digitalized Hungarian databases are accessible from abroad just as easily as Hungarian pipers can access foreign pipers' homepages and internet archives, leading to communication, data exchange, as well as institutional cooperation between them.

Bagpipe Education: Beginnings and Institutialization

The beginning of teaching might well have been the moment when the first revival pipers started to pass on in an institutional form what they had learnt from first-hand performers, from audio recordings and through

11 In the online database of the fieldwork recordings *Folklore Database* there are 3016 bagpipe recordings as a result of fieldwork 1988–2011. http://www.hagyomanyokhaza.hu/main/mediatar/adatbazisok/folklordokumentumok (accessed 23 May 2012). In the online database of all archive and revival published recordings *Published audio recordings* there are 374 bagpiper's ones. http://www.hagyomanyokhaza.hu/main/mediatar/adatbazisok/hangzokiadvanyok (accessed 23 May 2012).

12 From 297 music transcriptions of the archive bagpipe recordings of the Ethnographical Museum. 28 recordings can be downloaded in mp3. http://www.neprajz.hu/emir/ari/talalatok.php? (accessed 23 May 2012).

13 From 6000 recordings in the internet database of the Institute for Musicology; 85 are of bagpipe music which can be downloaded in mp3. http://db.zti.hu/24ora/dalok.asp (accessed 23 May 2012).

their own experimenting. It has been characteristic of Hungarian folk music education from the outset that it has mingled exact, scholarly methods quite fruitfully with the living, imitational (or instinctive) methods of learning that is well-known in folk tradition. Naturally, we will find similar methods in the practice of folk music education in other countries, with obviously differences due to the different circumstances. Bagpipe teaching in Bulgaria or in Scotland for instance has long been institutionalized and has used classical music school methods: the bagpipe is available in the same quality as are classical instruments, and pupils learn playing from sheet music, from professional teachers and play at an equally high level both on classical and folk instruments. Bagpipe culture in these countries, we have to admit, has long existed and on the soil of this thriving tradition the forms of institutional education could be established much sooner and more self-evidently. The Hungarian teachers of folk music education, however, still have to work with their own method shaped alongside personal experience and cannot rely on proper literature. In most places, teachers otherwise active as performers prepare their own schedule, using a first-grade art education document called *Basics of Folk Music* (Gelencsér 1994) or other experimental reference books and, through their own experiences and whatever audio recordings of folk music they find, they focus on the skills of the student in front of them. From the beginners' level to the academy, a common feature of these methods is that they are centred on the audio recordings, but make use of the performers' video recordings as well, and urge pupils to study folk music in its original environment (Kiss 2006: 76). The basis of the whole training therefore is that the student should acquire the musical mother tongue as perfectly as possible and, on these grounds, with the aid of studying musical theory and history of music, should develop the knowledge of the instrument—technique, virtuosity and personality—into a level of artistry.

From the year 1981 an employee of the Centre for Culture and Education of Somogy County, József Csíkvár began organising what he called "bagpipe schools," a series of regular courses in piping for young people, taught during summer and winter holidays at various cultural centres throughout the county. The program promoted the formation of study partnerships, whereby a more experienced piper took a newly arrived student under his or her wing. The pair would then practice together for days until the novice had learned not only the traditional tunes, but also the techniques of tuning and reed-making.

The bagpipe schools started a series of passing on and receiving, as many of Sándor Csoóri Jr.'s pupils—e.g. István Adorján, Zoltán Juhász, György Lányi and Kálmán Sáringer—themselves became teachers in turn. It was Sándor Csoóri Jr. who first produced a pipers' tune collection, shaping the teaching method along practical experience (Csoóri Jr. 1986).

The other form of institutional teaching was the "C category" folk music teacher's training organized in the early 1980s by the Folk Music Department at the Institute of Education where, besides practical training, participants received knowledge of folk music theory and ethnography and those passing the examinations successfully at the end of the course received an official certificate. This was important as folk musicians had to own such an official paper proving their qualification to be able to receive payment for their performances. Before this, the only such document available for the first generation of folk musicians rising to be "professionals" by the mid-1980s was a certificate issued by the National Light Music Centre (Országos Szórakoztatózenei Központ, "OSZK") or the National Stage Office (Országos Rendezőiroda "ORI"), where performers and music teachers with no understanding of peasant music were in charge of deciding the quality of dance hall musicians and ensembles, even determining the wages they could be paid.

The Special Institutions of Bagpipe Education – Folk Music Schools

After the change of the regime, there were dedicated folk music schools formed in many places. Out of these, besides the 3rd District State Music Schools' above mentioned department, which became a separate institute in 1991 under the name of Hungarian Folk Music School in Óbuda, we have to mention the Folk Music Department formed at the Kálmán Nádasdy Art School in 1988. Since their establishment, out of the 3 or 4 thou-

Fig. 3: Participants of a bagpipe camp. The third man from the right is Sándor Csoóri. Kaposvár, 1982. Photo: unknown photographer.

sand pupils studying in the two schools, about a hundred have learned to play the bagpipe.

As for teaching, a new phase began with the opening of the music and folk music department at Nyíregyháza's György Bessenyei Teacher Training College in 1990. This has been the first school where the teachers of folk music could obtain the higher degree necessary under current laws for teaching. In the beginning, many performers and folk music teachers enrolled at the college, lacking the necessary knowledge in music theory (solmisation), or simply in need of a document for their career. Although it is still possible to evade the law prescribing proper qualification, those for instance entitled "the Young Master of Folk Art" and having a teacher's or ethnographer's university degree can teach at a primary level of folk music education, yet musicians with an excellent mastery of the instrument and even skills in teaching but lacking the necessary degree are being forced out of the education. Many pipers, like István Berán, Tibor Okos, Lajos

Bergics or Zoltán Papp, have obtained a degree at the college. But the "father master" of the Hungarian bagpipe revival, Sándor Csoóri, does not have any official qualification, and the other excellent teacher of music, György Lányi, many of whose pupils have themselves become teachers, left the college after two terms.

With the folk music teachers' training at the college, the nationwide network of primary level education could be enlarged and, what is just as important, the institutions for a secondary level of folk music education could also be established. The profession of the "folk musician," with the classification of the instrument and the branch, was included in the "official national list of vocations" (Országos Képzési Jegyzék, "OKJ") in 1993. This document prescribes in detail what general theoretical requirements and, according to

Fig. 4: Group of Hungarian bagpipers in the bagpipe festival. The last Hungarian traditional bagpiper and bagpipers of different ages played together. Eger, 2000. Photo: István Berán.

the individual instrument, what practical requirements someone qualified as a secondary level folk musician should meet, as well as naming the spheres of activity that can be fulfilled with such a qualification.

Ferenc Kiss assumes that folk music is taught in two thirds of the 800 primary level art schools that exist in Hungary (Kiss 2006: 76). We have no data concerning the number of bagpipe departments in these schools, but would estimate it to be between 20 and 30, which shows a great leap in progress since the beginnings. In 2006, folk music was taught in four secondary music schools, and "folksong" or "folk music" became an accepted subject in general secondary music schools, which has helped to bridge the old gap between classical and folk musicians.

The crown of this process was when in 2007, folk music teacher training began with 20 students at Ferenc Liszt University of Music (Music Academy). Receiving a university level has restored folk music's reputation previously gained by the Folk Music Researcher Department, hallmarked by the names of Zoltán Kodály and László Lajtha, and established within the Musicology Department in 1951. In a discussion organized by long-established foreign high-level folk music schools in 2008, the "Hungarian model" turned out to be unique for several reasons. While in Northern and Western-European countries it was the university teaching of folk music that generated the market, in Hungary it happened the other way round. We have an already existing and very serious market which has called for its qualified experts. We do not have to present and look for folk music with all our might. It is a living and enlivening medium, if only for a few. At the moment there are two pipers studying at the Music Academy under Zoltán Juhász. They represent very well the two ways of entering high level education.

BAGPIPE RESEARCH

Music history and ethnomusicology research in Hungary have paid relatively little attention to bagpipe playing. For the revival pipers it was a couple of important studies dealing with the Hungarian bagpipe and pipers that offered crucial theoretical guidance and practical help. Besides Bartók's, Madarassy's, and Manga's writings, it was for instance Lajos Vargyas's study in music history, the bagpipe chapter in Bálint Sárosi's handbook (Sárosi 1967), Füzes's and Békefi's studies rich in details about the instrument technique that were useful to pupils wishing to learn.[14]

After a couple of years, the young pipers followed in the great researchers' footsteps and endeavoured to increase the scholarly results concerning the bagpipe. They started investigating in every part of the Hungarian language area to search for data about the instrument or actual instruments or old pipers still around. Expanding the research in time and space, many of them examined the morphology of bagpipe types, the role of bagpipe music, the beliefs concerning the bagpipe; and beside the practical experiments, many valuable works of ethnography and history were penned by the members of the young piper generation. The first important issue was Sándor Csoóri Jr.'s collection of bagpipe music aimed as a methodology

Fig. 5: One of the books published by Zoltán Szabó. ("A duda. The Bagpipe," Budapest: Néprajzi Múzeum, 2004). Photo: Katalin Juhász.

14 For the detailed bagpipe research history with the complete bibliography see Szabó 2006a.

handbook (1986), to be followed by Zoltán Juhász's monograph written on two traditional pipers, published with an audio supplement (1994, 1998). József Kozák published short comparative historic-geographical writings (e.g. 2004a, 2004b, 2005a, 2005c), Gyula Hankóczi (1998a, 1998b, 2007), Gábor Nagy (1999) and Aurél Szakál (1991–92, 1992, 1931) wrote about bagpipes and pipers in the Great Hungarian Plain, Péter Tanai (1995) and Iván Nagy (2002) about those in the Csallóköz, Zoltán Szabó about Serbo-Croatian bagpipes (e.g. 1991, 2001b) and pipers in Hungary (2004, Hála and Szabó 2010). Gergely Agócs edited a book (2001) including his own studies as well as Péter Éri's study on the historical naming of the bagpipe, József Kozák's on the prevalence of the Carpathian Basin bagpipe type, Ferenc Tobak's on pipers in Moldavia, and Zoltán Szabó's on Southern Slav bagpipe types. We have to emphasize Zoltán Juhász's multidisciplinary researches, in which for instance he dealt with the possible improvement of phonograph recordings (1995), and the ethnomusicological adaptation of artificial intelligences (2000, 2002, 2006, 2007). These latter examinations, through the structural analysis of tunes by mathematical methods, helped to place our previous knowledge concerning the regularities in the origin of tune-variations and the geographical diffusion of the variants into a new dimension. Another significant result was the Museum of Ethnography's exhibition arranged by Zoltán Szabó and the accompanying bi-lingual catalogue (Szabó 2004), which was acknowledged by international scholarship (Cheape 2007).

BAGPIPE MANUFACTURE

Bagpipe Manufacture in the First Period

In the beginning, it was extremely difficult to get hold of an instrument necessary for piping, as the old shepherd pipers' instruments were not really kept in good repair, in usable condition, nor did they meet the stricter demands of the stage at all. So someone wishing to play in a dance house or on stage had to acquire a proper instrument first. This could be done in several ways: either he tried to manually repair the instrument or its components he had received from elderly pipers or bought abroad or, copying the old instrument, he tried to manufacture a new one. For this, however, no-one had the necessary knowledge or experience at the time; neither did they have any specific tools.

After the initial experimenting, it soon turned out that only a few of the pipers were able to make a complete bagpipe, and all the others tried to get their instruments from them. Yet even these successful bagpipe manufacturers had to experiment a lot before they managed to prepare acceptable and reliable instruments. The best instrument measurements of this initial era were worked out by József Kozák and at the same time by the team of Sándor Csoóri Jr. and Ferenc Tobak. "Starting in the 1980s, Sándor Csoóri and I made several dozen bagpipes together in my shop in Veszprém. These were mostly straight-horned, Palóc types decorated with brass ferrules and inlay, though we also made a few lead-inlay instruments. Most of these latter pieces ended up in Western Europe, where people could pay for the time-consuming work involved. Later, I found myself walking my own path in instrument making. I based chanter dimensions on museum pieces, and later experiments and developments worked to refine the forms I used. By the second half of the 1980s, I was making instruments on my own, pipes that looked like the ones from the Palóc community of Kishartyán. I adopted elements from the experiences of French bagpipe makers in planning my drones, and elements of Bulgarian and Scottish bagpipe making in carving my reeds. I have a large collection of technical drawings of European bagpipes. It's gratifying to see how followers use the design practices and chanter forms I developed in making new bagpipes."[15]

The process of relearning bagpipe craftsmanship was accompanied almost from the start by a process of modernisation. Major innovations primarily involved the various bores, reeds (elder, cane, clarinet reeds lashed to metal inserts, and lately plastic blades made of an audio cassette box

15 Ferenc Tobak, personal communication with Katalin Juhász, September 2009. Ferenc Tobak's list of awards includes first prize at the National Folk Art Exposition in Nyíregyháza in 1985, the title of "Folk Applied Artist" as an instrument maker in 1992, and the "Pomegranate Award" at the *Twelfth National Folk Art Exposition* in Budapest in 1996.

or a piece of decorator cane fixed to a cane staple etc.), and leather curing process. Later, improvements were made to facilitate tuning. Every single alteration and innovation resulted in better quality bagpipe playing.[16]

Bagpipe Manufacture as it is Today

While in the early 1990s bagpipe makers strived to lift all the elements of bagpipe manufacture from the mystical to the rational, often relying on the results of their own haphazard experimenting, today we have exact technology complete in all its details. Following the time-honoured practice of old guild masters, Hungarian craftsmen have been inclined to study professional foreign instrument makers' methods so as to be able to make the best instruments themselves. The exchange of information is mutual,

Fig. 6: Pál Gadányi, the last Croatian traditional bagpiper and bagpipe maker living in Hungary. Tótújfalu, 2002. Photo: Zoltán Szabó.

16 For a much more detailed description of bagpipe making innovations see Juhász and Szabó 2010: 209–213.

Fig. 7: Andor Végh and Balázs Szokolay Dongó are making a bagpipe together (Bóly, 2007). Photo: Mátyás Bolya.

and the distinguished bagpipe manufacturers all over Europe are aware of one another's achievements.[17]

Bagpipe makers experiment with new materials all over the world; especially plastics have grabbed the imagination of the extremely creative, often playful constructors. Besides utopian ideas, there are many that can be applied in everyday life, for instance József Kozák's invention of children's bagpipe with a rubber bag, or the cheap practice instruments functioning with a membrane.[18] The electronic bagpipe, another great idea of bagpipe

17 We have quite a few examples for this as to a certain extent we also participate in this international circulation of information and personal networking. See e.g. Lundberg 2007.

18 We have come across many versions of plastic bagpipes. Some examples can be seen: www.hermandewit.be (Belgian Flemish bagpipe maker Herman Dewit), accessed 4 March 2009; www.dennishavlena.com (crazy plastic bagpipes of Dennis Havlena, Michigan, USA), accessed 4 March 2009.

manufacturers, has also been accomplished worldwide.[19] In Hungary, the electronic bagpipe is István Adorján's invention (Adorján's Hungarian Electronic Bagpipe), which is the best instrument for absolute beginners wishing to learn tunes. "Its nickname is electronic goat, and indeed, it has the sound of a bagpipe. On the chanter there are copper tubes in the place of the finger holes, and the sound is made by touch, and in the box replacing the bag there are the loudspeaker, the modulator and the tuner" (Ditzendy 2005). Its great advantage is that the pitch can be changed in a wider range, and more kinds of chanters can be fitted to the basic device.

CONCLUSION

The in-depth study of the activity of the Hungarian bagpipe-revival movement representatives clearly reveals that most of those dealing with the bagpipe are active in at least two of these roles (doer-maker or doer-knower), and many of them in all the three (doer-knower-maker). This complexity of diverse skills is what is revealed from this review of the revival of the bagpipe in Hungary. This complexity of skills needs to be emphasised.

The topic of this book, *Trapped in Folklore?* presumes a certain closeness. The Hungarian dance house movement including the bagpipe revival is not characterized by closeness as its essence is the opposite. We are not trapped in a "fossilized" tradition which has lost its function a long time ago, but we are open for novelties and we provide free passage between the authentic (old, traditional, nowadays hardly live) folklore and the men of today (modern culture). We study and document the folklore thoroughly and systematically. On the other hand we teach the traditional music as a "mother tongue" using the archives that are open for the public and transforming the data into auxiliary material. Once learning this "language" anyone can express themselves freely, moreover he/she may mix it with other "langua-

19 For example the Swedish Fagerstrom Technochanter, the Fagerstrom Technopipe, the Canadian electronic bagpipe by Ross Technologies, the hand-made MacPipe, made by William McGregor, and the German Deger Pipes (www.hotpipes.com/epipe.html; accessed 4 March 2009).

ges," too. Thus, the combination of tradition and creativity results in a large spectrum in instrument manufacturing and in the music, too.[20]

It is remarkable that it was the bagpipe's revival and further improvement that ran a similar course in many European countries. Another characteristic is that while in the beginning everybody stayed within their own scope (within their national borders), soon an international network was developed, in which the most distinguished bagpipe players, researchers and manufacturers of each country (often one person in several roles) came to be aware of one another, and beside learning about one another's achievements, they have applied them, and have often formed personal (friendly) relationships. This network of information and relations have brought together a "company" that can be seen as a peculiar subculture. Beyond the thorough analysis of the bagpipe revival in each country, a comprehensive research investigating this international "subculture" could also be illuminating.

Although the folk music revival has been studied in every country of the former East European block, and some of the musicians attending festivals (especially pipers) got to know one another well, we still know little of the actual process of how folk music was re-explored in these countries. A comprehensive and comparative international research (Juhász 1999), pointing far beyond the culture of folk revival, could certainly be highly informative.

20 We present more detailed interpretation and the styles of the bagpipe music in the article: Juhász and Szabó 2010.

REFERENCES

Agócs, Gergely (ed.)
2001 *A duda, a furulya és a kanásztülök: a magyar hangszeres zene folklórja.* Budapest: Planétás Kiadó.

Balogh, Balázs, and Ágnes Fülemile
2008 Cultural Alternatives, Youth and Grassroots Resistance in Socialist Hungary. The Folk Dance and Music Revival. *Hungarian Studies* 22 (1–2): 43–62.

Cheape, Hugh
2007 Critical review. Szabó Zoltán: A Duda, the Bagpipe. *Review of Scottish Culture* 19: 121–123.

Csoóri, Sándor, Jr. (ed.)
1986 *Dudanóták gyűjteménye. Énekelt dallamok. Módszertani segédanyag.* Kaposvár: Somogy Megyei Művelődési Központ.

Ditzendy, Attila Arisztid
2005 *A dudás a csárdából. Hangszer és Zene.* http://www.hzo.hu/vzp/index.dw?mit=131&vzp_kezmu_id=8&kezd=5&vzp_kezmu_kat_id=2 (accessed 4 Oktober, 2010).

Gelencsér, Ágnes
1994 *Magyar Népzenei alapismeretek.* Budapest: Calibra.

Hála, József, and Zoltán Szabó
2010 *Dudásoknak, kanászoknak közzibül, közzibül... A dudáról és dudásokról az ipolysági kanászhangversenyszázadik évfordulója alkalmából.* Budapest: Timp.

Hankóczi, Gyula
1998a Tárgyak és amiről nem beszélnek. Az alföldi duda emlékeiből. *Ethnographia* 109 (1): 147–158.

1998b XX. századi dudások Csongrád megyében és szomszédságában. *A Móra Ferenc Múzeum Évkönyve* 2: 167–185.

2007 *Foszlányok az alföldi duda történetéből.* Budapest: Timp.

Juhász, Katalin

1993 Nem úgy van most, mint volt régen... A táncházi folklorizmus néhány mai jelensége. In: Tóth Ferenc (ed.), *Népi kultúra mai környezetben. Fiatal Néprajzkutatók Országos Konferenciája.* 1991. (A Makói Múzeum Füzetei 75.) Makó: József Attila Múzeum, 82–93.

1999 *Folklore and Folklorism in Belgium,* 1999. *Final Report. Panta Rhei International Project UK.* Manuscript. Táncház - Archive House of Tradition, Budapest.

2011 Tevékenységformák és interpretációk modelljei: hagyomány és tudomány; hagyomány és kreativitás. In: Diószegi, László, and Katalin Juhász (eds.), *Hagyomány – Örökség – Közkultúra. A magyar népművészet helye és jövője a Kárpát-medencében.* Budapest: Teleki László Alapítvány, 157–166.

Juhász, Katalin, and Zoltán Szabó

2010 Rediscovery of the Bagpipe in Hungary. In: Hoppál, Mihály (ed.), *Sustainable Heritage.* Budapest: European Folklore Institute, 201–226.

Juhász, Zoltán

1994 *Kukucska Ernő nógrádi dudás és furulyás hagyatéka.* (Népzenei füzetek.) Budapest: Magyar Művelődési Intézet.

1995 Tone restoration of early phonograph recordings by adaptive multichannel system. In: Erényi, István (ed.), COMBIO'95: *Summer Workshop on Computational Modeling and Imaging in Biosciences, 28.–30. aug. 1995. Kecskemét.* (KFKI-1995-14/ M-H). Budapest: KFKI, 79–85.

1998 *Az utolsó dudás, Pál István nógrádi pásztor zenei öröksége.* (Népzenei füzetek.) Budapest: Magyar Művelődési Intézet.

2000 Contour Analysis of Hungarian Folk Music in a Multidimensional Metric Space. *Journal of New Music Research* 29 (1): 71–83.

2002 The Structure of an Oral Tradition. Mapping of Hungarian Folk Music to a Metric Space. *Journal of New Music Research* 31 (4): 295–310.

2006 A systematic comparison of different European folk music traditions using self-organising maps. *Journal of New Music Research* 35 (2): 95–112.

2007 Analysis of Melody Roots in Hungarian Folk Music Using Self-Organizing Maps with Adaptively Weighted Dynamic Time Warping. *Applied Artificial Intelligence* 21 (1): 35–55.

Kiss, Ferenc

2006 Számvetés – a népzenei mozgalom három évtizede. In: Sándor, Ildikó (ed.), *A betonon is kinő a fű.* Budapest: Hagyományok Háza, 67–108.

Kozák, József

2004a Egy alföldi duda világjárása. *Folkmagazin* 11 (2): 37.

2004b Dudafej, dudabőr. A magyar duda és a hangszer európai fejlődése. *Folkmagazin* 11/6: 38–39.

2005a Két bordósípos dudák Európában. *Folkmagazin* 12 (1): 40–41.

2005b A mi dudánk. *Folkmagazin* 12 (2): 27.

2005c Bőrduda – bordó. *Folkmagazin* 12 (3): 30.

Lányi, György (ed.)

2001 Magyar dudások. *Archív dudazene*. Budapest: Téka Foundation.

Lundberg, Dan, et al.

2003 *Music – Media – Multiculture. Changing Musicscapes.* Stockholm: Svensk visarkiv.

Lundberg, Dan

2007 *Bjårskpip* in Blossom. On the Revitalization Process of a Folk Music Instrument. *STM-Online* vol. 10; http://musikforskning.se/stmonline/vol_10/lundberg/index.php?menu=3 (accessed 17 Oktober 2010).

Nagy, Gábor

1999 Néhány gondolat a 'szögedi bűrdudáról'. *A Dugonics Társaság Évkönyve*: 267–279.

Nagy, Iván

2002 *A csallóközi dudáshagyomány*. Pozsony: Kalligram.

Sárosi, Bálint

1967 *Die Volksmusikinstrumente Ungarns. Handbuch der Europäischen Volksmusikinstrumente,* Serie I. Band I. Leipzig: Deutschler Verlag für Musik.

1980 (1998) *Hungarian Instrumental Folk Music.* Budapest: Hungaroton, LPX18045–7 (HCD 18236–37). (LP)

Stuber, György

2002 *Csángó-Hungarian bagpipers in Moldavia.* Budapest: Etnofon. ED-CD 053. (CD)

Szabó, Zoltán

1991 Dudások a magyarországi szerb és horvát népszokásokban. In: Halász, Péter (ed.), *A Duna menti népek hagyományos műveltsége, Tanulmányok Andrásfalvy Bertalan tiszteletére.* Budapest: Néprajzi Társaság. 459–466.

2001a Gajde és dude… Dudák és dudások a magyarországi horvátoknál és szerbeknél. In: Agócs, Gergely (ed.), *A duda, a furulya és a kanásztülök, A magyar hangszeres zene folklórja.* Budapest: Planétás Kiadó. 457–476.

2001b Gajde su gajde… Gajdaši i dudaši u Hrvata u Mađarskoj. *Etnografija Hrvata u Mađarskoj* 8: 105–122.

2004 *A duda/The Bagpipe* (A Néprajzi Múzeum tárgykatalógusai 9). Budapest: Néprajzi Múzeum.

2005 Bagpipes and bagpipers in the Carpathian Basin and beyond. *Hungarian Heritage* 6: 88–93.

2006a Bartók's bagpipers. *Hungarian Heritage* 7: 19–25.

2006b 'Elindultam hosszú útra' Egy társadalmi csoport utazásai a 20. század utolsó évtizedében. In: Sándor, Ildikó (ed.), *A betonon is kinő a fű.* Budapest: Hagyományok Háza, 161–182.

Szabó, Zoltán, and Krisztina Pálóczy (eds.)

2004 *Aki dudás akar lenni / Whoever Wants to Become a Piper.* Budapest: Néprajzi Múzeum. (CD)

Szakál, Aurél
1991–92 Emberfejes dudafejek a Dél-Alföldön. A Móra Ferenc Múzeum Évkönyve 1: 153–176.

1992 Dudások a Dél-Alföldön 1700-1860 között. In: Viga, Gyula (ed.), Kultúra és tradició I-II. *Tanulmányok Ujváry Zoltán tiszteletére.* Miskolc: Herman Ottó Múzeum, 335–342.

1993 Dudatípusok a Kárpát-medencében. Az Alföld és a szomszédos területek dudatípusai. In: Tóth, Ferenc (ed.), *Népi kultúra mai környezetben. Fiatal Néprajzkutatók Országos Konferenciája.* 1991. (A Makói Múzeum Füzetei 75.) Makó: József Attila Múzeum, 179–199.

2001 Dudások a Közép-Tisza vidéken. *Tisicum* 12: 257–264.

Tanai, Péter
1995 Sós Antal és dudái. *A Xántus János Múzeum és a Győr-Sopron Megyei Múzeumok Évkönyve Arrabona* 34: 321–371.

David Verbuč

FROM TEXT TO CONTEXT: PERFORMANCE EVENTS AMONG PRIMOŽ VILLAGERS IN NORTH SLOVENIA

ABSTRACT

In this paper, I look at how Primož villagers from North Slovenia, in the years 2000 and 2001, utilized folklore texts in their performances, and how their performances were sequenced. I discuss the functions of these performances and how cultural values and meanings were reflected and generated through them. My aim is not only to show some of the salient characteristics of Primož village music performances, but also to emphasize that there is an important difference between textual and contextual approaches to the study of people's lore and practices.

Key words: ethnography of performance, place and space, music/culture relationships, Slovenian village music

INTRODUCTION

In this paper, I focus on a small group of villagers from Primož, North Slovenia, and their social events, analyzing them as performances. Specifically, I look at how Primož villagers utilized folklore texts in their performances, in the years 2000 and 2001, when I was doing my field work research there (with some additional observations in 2008), and how they sequenced their performances. Furthermore, I discuss the functions of these performances, their spatial aspects, and how cultural values and meanings were reflected and generated through them. In the beginning of the paper, I additionally present some of the general characteristics and issues related to the village music from Primož at that time. My aim is not only to show some of the salient characteristics of Primož village music performances, and thus to present my findings from my field research there, but also to emphasize that there is an important difference between textual and contextual approaches to the study of people's lore and practices, and to promote the latter over (and in conjunction with) the former.[1] When discussing performances in Primož, I am mostly focusing on name-day celebrations and similar, convivial and small group, events that I attended there.

Primož is a sparsely populated village of around one hundred and sixty inhabitants which stretches North West of the town Ljubno over the Primož hill in the mountainous region of northern Slovenia. In the research that I started in 2000, I worked with a particular extended family and its relatives, neighbours, and friends from Primož (I will call this group Primož villagers). Besides collecting folk songs in Primož and in the wider region of the Upper Savinja Valley, I also started attending the social events of Primož villagers, to do an intensive, context-sensitive research with participant-observation as a main method of inquiry. I felt there was and mainly still is a lack of this kind of ethnographic scholarly work among Slovenian ethnomusicologists and music folklorists (there are some exceptions among younger Slovenian scholars), who, when it comes to Slovenian folklore, instead typically collect and analyze folk songs and tunes, and interview informants outside of their social contexts.[2] I was especially interested in when, how, where, why, and by whom folklore texts are used and performed. Consequently, I felt the need to focus on performance and process, not only on texts, for an emphasis on textual analysis can obscure the social life of folklore—the meanings and functions they bear and acquire in specific social contexts and occasions.

1 Things are more complicated than this. Contextual can be studied, and interpreted, as textual, i.e. culture as text (cf. Geertz 1973, Geertz 1983), while textual can be studied not only in relation to its content, form, or historical context, but also as a part and parcel of a wider discursive (ideological or epistemological) context, or as a cultural discourse in itself—as a text embodying the context (for instance in cultural studies or critical theory).

2 There are still other methodological and ideological "trappings" of folklore research in Slovenia and elsewhere. For instance, this kind of folklore approach also neglects the role and shape of village music in the present. There is also a lack of interest in other (ethnic) types of folklore in Slovenia, and/or in (other) more contemporary forms of people's lore and practice (that are perhaps not related to older Slovenian folk traditions, like various urban phenomenon). Both exist outside of the frame of Slovenian national cultural politics that have a significant impact on Slovenian (mostly institutional) scholarship.

PRIMOŽ CULTURE BETWEEN CULTURAL REPRESENTATION AND VILLAGE PRACTICE

Observing Primož villagers and their social events, I noticed certain general characteristics. As with any social group, Primož villagers are not a bounded or isolated community. Through their interaction with their surroundings, they organized or participated in at least three types of social events: their intimate inner-community (or in-group) events, that were located in the "core" of their social world (cf. Bohlman 1988), events that involved the neighboring villagers, or were organized there, and events in the nearby town Ljubno or even farther away in the region, on the "boundary" of their social world (ibid.), where they participated in various occasions that were mostly staged, tourist, folklore, or entertainment events (see Verbuč 2009b). Bohlman discusses concepts of "core" and "boundary" in terms of "identity" (Bohlman 1988: xviii, 62–67), which can lead to essentialist or "expressionist" interpretations of identity (cf. Butler 1990). In contrast, I understand these two terms as spatial concepts that are related to different performative practices of Primož villagers, and also to emotional and political aspects of their lives.

I consider "everyday" and celebratory village practices in opposition to "staged" events. While "staged" folklore events could be seen as a part of everyday life, they are also separated from it, as a "time out of time" and as "place out of place" (cf. Kozorog 2011), "dislocated" practices that become "symbols" in themselves (DaMatta 1991: 69, 70). In regard to Primož villagers, staged folklore events represent a temporal break from their everyday working activities (a "time out of time"), and a spatial representation of their dislocated "core" cultural practices on the "boundary" of their social lives (a "place out of place"). While Kozorog discusses festivals as "place[s] in the space" (Kozorog 2011) that are about recognition and branding (as tourist and commercial events), I see individual staged folklore representations of Primož villagers as "place[s] out of place," that were, following the rules and norms of folklore events, more about standardized and selective representations and appropriations of difference. In terms of the emotional aspects, Primož villagers often stressed that cultural activities in their village, and more specifically in their homes, were the ones that they valued the most. On the other hand, they not only represented their traditions on the stages outside of their village ("place out of place"), but also succeeded in (re)creating their own cultural practices and spaces outside of their village through occasional self-initiatives and informal singing and dancing activities in Ljubno. Primož villagers thus asserted their autonomy over their performances and their cultural life, and occasionally managed to (re)create a "place in the space," not as a tourist branding, but as a political claim to space.

In regard to their "core" activities, Primož villagers organized most of their in-group social events in their homes, which was an important influence on the continuity of their traditions (cf. Slobin 2000: 47, for a similar assessment related to house parties and the continuity of old time music tradition in the US, in the 1930s and 1940s). Primož villagers retained various traditional forms of family and in-group, everyday and celebratory activities (marriages, name-day celebrations, caroling, and certain para-liturgical and after-work village events), which in their modified and contemporary forms suited their social and cultural needs. Besides, approximately in the last four decades, they have adapted and started practicing other forms of social events such as lighting bonfires and celebrations on New Year eve and birthdays.

Traditional life and folk music among Primož villagers existed in the beginning of the 2000s in a transformed form, as a modification of their older cultural and social practices.[3] National, regional, and local institutions, scholars, and cultural workers stimulate, promote, and organize staged folklore and tourist representations of past folklore "texts", customs, songs and tunes, and thus impose their comprehension of the past traditions on many participants who, often thus subsequently "trapped by folklore," live and traverse between their vital community traditions on one side and the condensed and manufactured traditions on the other (cf. Šivic 2007). The obvious paradox of these shifting identities is that on the stage, at local

3 Cultural practices in Primož are changing to this day, as I observed during a few recent visits there.

cultural, tourist, and folkloric events in Ljubno, which were found "on the boundary" (Bohlman 1988) of the cultural and social life of the small peasant community of Primož villagers (and at the same time in the center of the local public sphere), folklore traditions, represented as "authentic," were selectively tailored for the need of these events (and were thus of mixed nature in themselves). Simultaneously, everyday and celebratory activities in Primož (at the "core" of their life) that could be called "authentic" (not controlled by outsiders), but are at the same time "hybrid" in their character (because of the many influences from national and transnational cultural spheres, for instance from Slovenian *narodno-zabavna* music, a type of pop-folk music; see Verbuč 2009a),[4] were often either misunderstood as "inauthentic" or entirely ignored. However, both, "core" and "boundary" activities, and "folklorist" and "on-the-ground" "authenticities" (or better "hybridities"; cf. Stokes 2004) are an important part of a "multidimensional" contemporary culture of Primož villagers (cf. Bohlman 1988: 135).

Attitudes toward "tradition" and "folklore texts" differ greatly between emic and etic perspectives. For many Slovenian villagers, these texts carry a functional value, while outsiders see them primarily in aesthetic or ideological (nationalist or romantic) terms, thus seeing the "Other [as] not really Other" (Žižek 2003). For instance, the songs that are most valued, and most often performed in Slovenian villages, might not have the same value for, or get the same attention from, scholars and collectors, who often look for more archaic songs.[5] Singing with the accompaniment of accordion is

---

4 Instrumental music of Primož villagers, and to a certain extent also their singing style and repertories, were greatly influenced by Slovenian *narodno-zabavna* music, a characteristic type of Slovenian pop-folk music, which was formed in the 1950s, with the Avsenik Brothers as its most prominent exponents. The style was derived directly from older (mostly North-Western and Central) Slovenian instrumental folk music traditions, was disseminated through Slovenian national mass media, and quickly became a marker of Slovenian national identity.

5 In Primož, for instance, they often perform songs that would not be considered archaic from the standpoint of musical folkloristics. These often entail sentimental and common (*navadne*) songs. In addition, while scholars and collectors often particularly value songs without any missing strophes, Primož villagers often sang songs in a

of a great value in many villages, while collectors and scholars usually try to avoid it on recordings (with an argument that such was the case in the past with traditional singing). The same goes for other singing or instrumental music styles, that differ between village contemporary music styles on the one hand, and the styles heard on Slovenian archival field recordings (recorded mostly outside cultural contexts), or styles of folklore or folk revival groups, on the other. However, with the outside recognition of their "traditions" (and lives) on the one hand, and through scholarly work on the other, these emic and etic perspectives started to shift. Primož villagers started recognizing or adding additional (aesthetic) value to their "traditions" and "texts" (cf. Slobin 2000: 20, on the "visibility" of traditions), thus also reviving them, or engaging in staged representations. On the other hand, outsiders will perhaps start to acknowledge villagers and their traditions and lives as a whole, inseparable from the folklore texts that they are transforming through their practices.

CONTEXTUALIZATION AND RECONTEXTUALIZATION OF FOLKLORE TEXTS

In a narrow sense, contextual performance of folklore text is sometimes understood as a type of performance when a text fits the event in content and function, for instance, wedding songs performed at weddings. In a wider sense, all folklore texts performed at any event are contextual. In that sense, re-contextualized text that is found outside of its expected context becomes part of another context and acquires and generates new meanings. For instance, tragic ballads can be performed at weddings, or wedding songs at casual singing events. By the same logic, any folklore text performed outside of the "primary" context, for instance at staged events, is contextual (cf. Ben-Amos 1993).[6] The only difference is in the types of contexts.

very fragmented manner, not only omitting the strophes, but sometimes only singing particular lines, or merging ("contaminating") them with other songs (see below).

6 In fact, staged context is for many performers their "primary" context of performance.

Besides the general social structure and cultural values, situational aspects that govern performances (cf. Ben-Amos 1993: 215, Turner 1987: 8, Bauman 1975: 299), and are shaped by them, there are also emergent qualities of the performance, "creative manipulations" (Bauman 1975: 300, 302–306), and individual choices and strategies, which bring in the element of indeterminacy (cf. Bauman 1975: 302, Turner 1987: 3, Duncan 1992, Béhague 1992). In Primož, songs were often used (re-contextualized) as "tools," or as "open-ended semantic codes" (Qureshi 1987: 80) for achieving certain functions, roles, or goals through performance. To paraphrase Clifford Geertz, meanings arise from the roles texts play in performance and what their import is (Geertz 1973: 17, 10), and not necessarily from their textual or semantic meaning (Ben-Amos 1971: 11, Bauman 1975: 292, Hufford 1995). Concomitantly, texts utilized in and through performance can bear and gain multiple meanings. In addition, in Primož, there was often an overlapping between "narrated" (textual) and "narrative" (contextual) events or meanings in performance (cf. Bakhtin 1981: 255),[7] when singers used songs or parts of songs to reference real-time situations (i.e. when they used or referenced "narrated" as "narrative").

For instance, in the course of performance, individual participants chose songs, or their musical or textual structure or content (themes, refrains or particular motives or lines from songs), which generated and enhanced particular experiences and moods, regardless of whether these same choices would otherwise fit the occasion. In regard to structure, they could choose

7 Bakhtin defines "narrated" as "the event that is narrated in the work" and "narrative" as "the event of narration itself" (Bakhtin 1981: 255). "Narrated" and "narrative" usually take place in different times and places (ibid.), except in the case of improvising the lyrics that are related to the situation, on the spot. In that case, "narrated" and "narrative" take place at the same time and place. Narrated can in that case sometimes function as a metacommentary of the narrative (commentary on the performance), for instance, through improvisation of songs that comment on the playing of the musicians or on the mood of the event. Alternatively narrative can function as a metacommentary on a narrative, for instance, with audience participation when the singing or instrumental playing is appreciated, or through non-participation, when it is not. In addition, narrative can also function as a metacommentary on the narrated (commentary on the content of songs), for instance, through any type of verbal comments, or non-verbal and emotional reactions to the content of the songs that are performed.

repetitive songs that enticed participation (see below), or utilized dense polyphonic (3–6 part) vocal textures to achieve the feeling of coherent unity. In regard to content, they often chose certain songs to express their individual feelings or assert their individual or group identity or emotions. Very commonly they sang songs that implicated joy, or nostalgia for lost youth or lost love. Individual singers often singled out a particular song as "my" song. Or they collectively (usually at the height of the event) sang a song "Mi smo pa fajn ljudje" (We are fine people), to express their contentment and pride, or a song "Mi se mamo radi" (We like each other), to emphasize their unity and love for each other. Individual participants chose specific songs to communicate specific messages: for example, men or women often started a song which asserted their masculinity or femininity. Some more assertive women thus, sometimes in a more or less obvious manner, initiated songs that on the surface did not seem particularly relevant to the situation, but included lines such as 'Why would you walk after me, 'You will not sleep with me anymore,' or '… and he is not here, and he doesn't have to be here.' Sometimes, they simultaneously asserted their peasant identity, by singing the song that contained a line 'If I will pick someone, he will be a peasant.' They either sang the whole song which contained only a brief allusion to a specific meaning, or only picked out these meaningful lines and sang them independently, sometimes in exchange with others who did the same.

Primož villagers often addressed specific individuals with songs and thus communicated specific meanings that would otherwise be communicated verbally. They toasted a person celebrating a name-day in the middle of the event, naming him or her in it, and thanking him or her as a host, for giving them food and wine. They did that once with a toasting song 'One tumbler of ripe wine / was walking up and down the table, / let's toast to Kumprej, / so he'll share his drink with us again next year.' One man thus replied with a song 'This is what it gives me pleasure, / that so many people sit around this table ...,' singing about how happy a person he is that there are so many people around the table that are drinking from their glasses. Other participants joined in singing these songs instantly, as if they were just ordinary songs. Only the emotion and the looks in their eyes were showing that there is a deeper meaning behind these choices and actions. Toward the end of the same event, guests sang to the host a farewell and thanksgiving song, starting with his name: 'Kumprej, stay healthy, / do not forget us, / we must go now.' At every event, Primož villagers sang similar songs at the beginning or ending of the event that would indicate their arrival or departure.[8] At the end, they often sang several songs in a row, or interpolated them between the others, especially when the atmosphere was very lively and the departing party could not really leave, even if they wanted to. The hosts, in collusion with those who were not yet willing to depart, were usually restraining them, either pouring them more wine, or holding them around their necks, and initiating song after song. This sometimes went on for one or even two hours, before people really started to leave.

In addition, Primož villagers often spurred resting musicians to play for dance, for instance, with a song "Muzikantje so sami zabušanjte, nečejo, da špilajo" (Musicians are all slackers, they don't want to play). With certain songs, they sometimes strove to control the flow of the singing with suddenly initiating a song "Pa te pesmi je preč, pa ne pojmo je več" (This song is over, let's not sing it anymore), while others still sang some long ballad. Or they educated and simultaneously teased a young girl with a song "Ko sem še pri mamici ležala" (While I still slept by my mother), that is about losing virginity, and very often, they taunted and prodded each other with various jocular songs. Toward that end, they sometimes improvised or paraphrased other songs for taunting with on the spot. Some of these taunting songs could be sung individually, but most of the songs were sung collectively, in multipart harmonies. There was only one person needed to start the song and lead it, and the others would join soon after.

8 In the beginning, they could sing songs like "Nocoj je en fajn večer" (Tonight is a fine night), "Dober večer, ljubca moja" (Good evening, my darling), or "Fantje se zbirajo"(Young lads are gathering). For the end, they would initiate and sing these songs: "Glažek še ni prazen" (This glass is not yet empty), "Sprajmo se" (Let's get going), "Zdaj smo delo dokončali" (Now, we finished the work), "To še spijemo, pa gremo" (Let's empty this one, and then we can go), "Ljubica, lahko noč" (My darling, good night), "Adijo, pa zdrava ostani" (Good bye, and stay healthy), or a song that contains a part 'How narrow is the path, / oh, when will I be home' (*Kak ozke so stezice, / oj kdaj bom pa jaz doma*).

Or if they did not, somebody else would initiate another song. Besides, all participants could choose songs, even if they did not know how to start and/or lead them—they could simply express their wishes, then somebody else would start it, and the rest would join in after first couple of words.

These practices reveal that many of the songs that Primož villagers sang had a utilitarian value, and simultaneously carried an aesthetic function that was also part of a social one. They most enjoyed singing multipart songs, that incorporated many if not all of the participants, and that were sung in a very coherent manner (connecting them socially through aesthetically unifying singing).

SEQUENCING OF PERFORMANCE EVENTS IN PRIMOŽ

Attending, observing and analyzing various Primož villagers' in-group social events, I noticed certain meaningful patterns of performance. Their performance events were heterogeneous, utilizing a plethora of performance types and genres. At one single event they often employed singing, dancing and instrumental playing, games, and various verbal practices such as telling jokes, taunting, or everyday talk. In relation to these characteristics, one older Primož woman, talking about the past, remembered: "There was all mixed together, there was always something happening." This was still true at many of their in-group Primož events that I attended. More specifically, Primož villagers typically performed all these genres in a very close succession, and in sequential patterns that alternated between many seemingly opposing binary categories.

Primož performances, like all performances, "draw on biological, climatic, ecological rhythms, as well on social rhythms, as models of the processual forms it sequentially employ[s] in its episodic structure" (Turner 1982: 81). Their events were thus organized in regard to season, calendar events, life cycle, working week, and daily activities, while performances in themselves, often reflected and generated, but also transgressed, inverted and with that consequentially affected, social structure and social values and norms.

Singing and instrumental playing with dancing represented the main festive activities in Primož, and alternation between them was quite regular, usually in terms of longer or shorter sets. At the beginning of the event or later on if the participants got tired or sleepy, some especially charismatic or capable performers initiated particular performance activities which enticed participation and connected people: special songs, for instance medleys of toasting songs, or circular songs such as "Tri krat tri je devet" (Three times three is nine), or "Kdor je januarja rojen bil" (Who is born in January), a special circle and participatory for all pillow-dance *pouštertanc*, or various social and entertaining games that often contained musical elements. In between, or sometimes simultaneously with other activities, people utilized many verbal folklore genres: anecdotes, jokes, witty comments, jests and puns. Certain events with ritual characteristics, mostly name-day celebrations and weddings but also other merrymaking performances, were usually "keyed" (Bauman 1975: 295–298) with special introductory, intermediary and concluding customs or acts.[9]

Regarding dances, there was a regular alternation between polkas and waltzes. Waltzes are slower so they offer a moment of rest between fast polkas and they are also, as folk musicians say, suitable for dancers to squeeze (*stiskati*) each other. Singing of older, more melancholic songs tended to be slower and in a rubato fashion while more jocular or bawdy songs were very often sung faster, with giusto rhythm. A lot of the newer songs that Primož villagers sang were also very dance-like and fast. In addition, women's songs alternated with men's, and occasionally sacred songs alternated with secular or profane. Informal parts of events alternated and were framed with formal ones and there was also an alternation of group formations: singing was usually performed in circles (standing in a *krenc*, i.e. garland, or sitting around the table or room) while dancing

9 These often included the following: singing of ritual songs, performances of introductory verbal formal speeches, or exploding firecrackers upon the arrival to the house. Events that were related to religious practices, such as the singing in the inn after a special perennial church mass event, were often "keyed" or marked with one or two sacred folk songs.

was usually performed in pairs (with the exception of a pillow-dance; see below).

Sequencing of melancholic or sad and happy or jocular songs was noticeable, but was usually not followed in strict and regular alternations and patterns. Occasionally, people alternated between them in close successions, one song after another, for a short period of time. More often, however, songs were performed in longer or shorter alternating sets. Sad and melancholic songs were more often but not necessarily performed at the beginning or at the end of the longer event. This particular sequencing and alternating of melancholic and happy songs also depended on other factors: on the nature and prevailing mood of the occasion (sometimes there was a more joyous atmosphere than at other times), on situational context or on an individual's selections of songs and the goals of those individuals during singing. However, alternating between these general moods was, no matter the variation in structure and sequence pattern, valued and desired. One folk musician said that after singing songs "for the hearth" or "soft songs," as he called more melancholic songs, he or other folk musicians or singers would often quickly switch the mood. When he was still playing, this was, as he said, "most appetizing," because there was so much "variation in mood." What is interesting in this list of oppositional binaries found in Primož performances is the manner of their juxtaposition: there were no strict boundaries between them in performance. Instead, musicians passed from one to another without a pause. In addition, they were not performed apart, in separate parts of events or even separate occasions, but were all part of the whole event.

Given that music and other cultural forms reflect and generate social relations, it is possible to draw a close connection between the structures and sequences of Primož villagers' performances and the "rhythm" (Turner 1982: 81) of their social life. For instance, it was very common to hear older Primož villagers say that life was, when they were young, on the one hand extremely hard, and on the other very joyful. One woman said to me: "[We] used to be joyful, although [we] had hard lives and suffered a lot, when we discarded our burdens, we immediately started to sing." Social and religious restrictions were in addition also very hard, so there were in the calendar cycle alternations between ordinary periods and on the other hand fasting periods where merrymaking was prohibited.[10] Finally, most of the peasants were very poor, but people always found something to put on the table and sacrificed their supplies for marriages, celebrations and other festive occasions. At the time, when I was doing my research in Primož, conditions were not drastically different. People in Primož mostly did not fast anymore, but they still lived modestly and worked very hard. Besides, their social and economic status and structure has not changed much and their way of life was a blend of traditional and contemporary—residual and emergent practices, customs, and values that went hand in hand in Primož. Oppositions between hard work and ecstatic pleasure, and deficiency and exuberance were to a greater or smaller degree still a part of Primož social reality.

Work for life and celebration of life, sadness and joy, sacred and profane, contemplation and physicality, singing and dancing, slow and fast, formal and informal, traditional and contemporary, and individual and communal were all part of one life and one community. Their events established that life can be full of contradictions that have to be accepted. The structure of their performance events reflected these contradictions and oppositions and promoted the balancing of extremes. Primož villagers depended on these oppositions, but at the same time on their balancing each other out through communal performance events. These events thus did not strive to eliminate those oppositions, but merely to establish them as necessary parts of everyday life, while simultaneously balancing their tensions.

In addition, binaries usually contain elements from their opposing sides, or there are also some forms that function as "mediators," that "synthesize" both sides (Lévi-Strauss 1955, Lévi-Strauss 1981: 74). For instance, while singing, Primož participants often swayed when in a special mood,

10 People for instance fasted four weeks before Christmas and forty days before Easter, which meant there was no merrymaking, singing or dancing during that time. Consequently, the first days after fasting, Saint Stephen's day on December 26, and Easter Monday, were important and highly anticipated happy events with lots of singing and dancing.

or, while dancing they exultantly sang short lines to instrumentally performed tunes, or engaged in short spontaneous exultant vocal utterances, called *juckanje*. As a "mediate" form, the only dance which was performed in Primož regularly with singing was the pillow-dance or *pouštertanc*. It additionally "synthesized" dancing in a circle alternated with dancing in couples in its two part form. Many folk songs that were performed at the events in Primož (and many Slovenian folk songs in general) also have an inherent oppositional or ambivalent structure of merriness versus melancholy, whether in the relationship, respectively, between melody and lyrics, or in the lyrics or in musical and textual form, for instance within the relation between A and B parts of the songs, or strophe and refrain (see also Kumer 1996: 79, 81). These "synthesized" forms not only bring together opposing forces, but also retain their dissonance, as a functional force in themselves.

NOTES ON FUNCTIONAL FACTORS, CULTURAL VALUES, AND ANTI-STRUCTURE

Alternation among different genres, types, and moods in performance had a socio-psychological effect on participants in Primož. Alternation between slow and fast performances, between dancing and singing and melancholic and joyous moods made events more dynamic and allowed for appropriate pacing that increased the endurance of participants and optimized the effects of performance. Primož people are restrained and rough on their surface, particularly because of their difficult living conditions. My assessment of the alternation of moods and activities at their events is that this specific sequentiality had a particular, therapeutic and social function for Primož villagers. Sad and contemplative songs first softened their moods and opened them emotionally, while joyous and lively songs and activities consequently enabled them to overcome troubled feelings and thus strengthen themselves, and at the same time connect themselves socially through active participation. This was a double-staged process that was at the same time individually therapeutic and socially connective, while simultaneously enabled participants to confront the "rhythm" and "structure" of their lives on the metaphoric and ritualistic level.[11]

One retired musician said that people there "cure their nerves" with singing. He said that you could recognize those who do not participate in singing (or other social activities) because they are usually in a bad mood. For him, singing raised the spirit and also induced the will to work.[12] To understand that such sequential performance juxtapositions were necessary for desired psychological states, let me quote another folk musician who told me, that at weddings, you have to sing sad songs, to make people cry. He added: "Sadness changes into happiness, and if this does not occur, there is no happiness."

This kind of pacing also lead to climactic releases of individual and collective energy and encouraged ecstatic, exultant and cathartic states of "forgetting" (people in Primož often said that with singing "we forget everything else"). Sequencing of oppositions in performance resulted in a heightened experience. When a certain enhanced mood was achieved at the events in which I participated, participants would often persist in it for a while, breaking the flow of oppositions and "fixed" (Bauman 1975: 297, Béhague 1992: 175) the structure and intensity of the performance for a

11 I understand metaphor as a "plan" or "organizing image" for a ritual or performance event to transform people, to "approximate subject to the metaphor" (Fernandez 1986: 43). Lakoff and Johnson argue that metaphors structure our actions (1980: 4). Primož performances functioned as metaphors of their social lives that approximated Primož villagers to the hardships and contradictions of their lives, and simultaneously to the conditions that helped them overcome them.

12 Slovenian psychologist Anton Trstenjak described in terms of this and similar oppositions the character and a special "Alpine sentimentality"of Slovenian Alpine people (of which Primož villagers are part of), which is not (in his questionable terms) "effeminate weakness," but rather special "tender sentimentality" (Trstenjak 1991). He talks about their "contradictory" characters, characterizing them as humble but hospitable, openhearted but restrained, and as people who, on the one hand, like to prod, tell jokes and are witty, but do not like to talk about their hard life, because they know this leads to self-pity, which kills the will to live (ibid.). It seems that Primož villagers communicated about their hard lives through songs, which, as "ritualized communication" (cf. Blacking 1973: 50), also protected them from exposing their personal feelings directly.

longer period (sometimes for thirty minutes, or even an hour). Only after a longer period, would they switch to another type of performance or change the mood.

Turner argues that communities during ritual or liminal states achieves a "dissolution of normative social structure" (Turner 1982: 28). The main characteristic of liminal states is to achieve a state of *communitas*, or of equality (Turner 1995: 96, 116), and its anti-structure, a temporarily reversed normative social structure that consequently generates cultural change (Turner 1982: 28). At a heightened moment of a name-day event, around midnight, Primož villagers started to sing a song "Mi se mamo radi" (We like each other), which included phrases: 'We like, like, like each other / like all of the night. // We like to sleep together / like all of the night. // We like to sing together / like all of the night. // Because we are all young / young all of the night.' While singing it, they immediately redirected the song, in an *attacca* fashion, into singing the words 'We drink everything, we spend everything, / and then we go home sober.' Here, Primož villagers reached and expressed coherence and unity and at the same time reverted their ordinary, everyday position: they all became, or at least felt, young and connected, and they even hinted that they could transcend what is otherwise unavoidable—becoming sober again after a whole night of drinking and singing. They created a "time out of time" and a "space within a place," a space of equality through singing and social interaction in the everyday place of hardship and hierarchical social relations. Primož villagers would also constantly invert serious love or tragic songs by changing words or phrases in a subtle and witty manner (for instance instead of singing 'When the dogs start barking' they sing 'When *we* dogs start barking'). When vigils for the dead were still held at their homes, they would sing marriage songs and play amusement games, but only after midnight.[13] People also regularly tended to communicate through song, rather than through speech, at these performance events, which additionally exemplified reversals of the normative, or the anti-structure. Besides,

13 There is an anecdote, that one man once even said, when asked, if people would rather stop singing at the vigil in his house: "don't stop singing, let there be at least once merriness in this house."

everybody, at least at certain heightened moments, became a competent singer and participant, from children to older people, no matter their social and economic status.

At seasonal and other rites in peasant societies, as Turner argues, liminal states "set people up [... and] elevate those of low status transiently before returning them to their permanent humbleness" (Turner 1982: 25; cf. Kapchan 1995: 482). At Primož events, people, at least temporarily, felt as though they became something else, reaching a state of *communitas* that elevated them, or carried them away from their ordinary and hard lives. For instance, when singing, Primož villagers said, "we forget everything else," "we feel like a family," or described themselves as "being rich." One woman said, it is "richness—to come together and to be in a good mood." "Richness," as a reversed and elevated social state of Primož villagers, was found not only in their feelings, but also on a structural level during their events: tables were "richly laden" with wine and food, events were "rich" with happenings and various genres of performances, of moods, verbal play and wittiness. Playing and singing was relatively "rich" with embellishments and the singing texture was always "rich"—thick, loud and full.[14] Even in the content of the songs, the subject of poverty was usually absent, or was sung about in a ironic manner. These reversals were in constant interplay with the normative and they gradually intensified through the sequencing of events.

CONCLUSION

My aims in this paper were threefold. First, I critiqued institutional and scholarly approaches to contemporary Slovenian village traditions. Second, I presented some of the characteristics of village musical culture in Primož, North Slovenia, and their performance events as observed during my research there, mostly in the years 2000, and 2001, and I proposed

14 As already noted, there was a tendency to sing in as many voices as possible—in some places in five or even six, although this was more common in the past.

some theoretical considerations of contemporary Slovenian village music practices. In that respect, I propose theoretical approaches (distinction between core and boundary practices, and issues of place and space) that underscore multidimensionality and complexity of contemporary cultural practices in Primož. Third, I am mostly concerned with performance events in Primož, and their structure, function, and meaning. In that respect, I observed practices of contextualizing and re-contextualizing folklore texts that emphasize how these texts can have very different, and sometimes opposing meanings and functions, when considered not as texts in themselves but as a part of performance events. Additionally, I focused on a specific sequential structure of performance events in Primož that oscillates between binary oppositions, and its specific cultural functions. Both cultural practices point to the need for reconsideration of folklore text not only as semantic and aesthetic entities (both different from emic or etic perspectives) but also, if not foremost, as means for specific social and socio-psychological ends for participants. Finally, I suggest specific interpretations of performance events in Primož that unveil the interrelation between music texts and performances on the one hand, and local social and cultural structure and values on the other. In this way, it is possible to recognize central values of singing and dancing for Primož villagers, of feelings of both, conviviality and jocularity on one hand, and melancholic sentimentality on the other, and of the metaphoric "richness" of either feeling, event, or musical texture.

REFERENCES

Barber-Keršovan, Alenka
1989 Tradition and Acculturation as Polarities of Slovenian Popular Music. In: Frith, Simon (ed.), *World music, politics and social change*. Manchester, New York: International Association for the Study of Popular Music, 73–89.

Bakhtin, Mikhail
1981 *The Dialogic Imagination*. Austin: University of Texas Press.

Bauman, Richard
1975 Verbal Art as Performance. *American Anthropologist* 77 (2): 290–311.

Béhague, Gerard Henri
1992 Music Performance. In: Bauman, Richard (ed.), *Folklore, Cultural Performances, and Popular Entertainment: A Communications-Centered Handbook*. New York: Oxford University Press, 172–178.

Ben-Amos, Dan
1971 Toward a Definition of Folklore in Context. *The Journal of American Folklore* 84 (331): 3–15.
1993 'Context' in Context. *Western Folklore* 52 (2–4): 209–226.

Blacking, John
1973 *How Musical is Man?* Seattle: University of Washington Press.

Bohlman, Philip V.
1988 *The Study of Folk Music in the Modern World*. Bloomington and Indianapolis: Indiana University Press.

Butler, Judith
1990 *Gender Trouble*. New York and London: Routledge.

DaMatta, Roberto
1991 *Carnivals, Rogues, and Heroes: An Interpretation of the Brazilian Dilemma.* Notre Dame/London: University of Notre Dame Press.

Duncan, Starkey Jr.
1992 Interaction, Face-to-Face. In: Bauman, Richard (ed.), *Folklore, Cultural Performances, and Popular Entertainment: a Communications-Centered Handbook*. New York: Oxford University Press, 21–28.

Fernandez, James W.
1986 *Persuasions and Performances: The Play of Tropes in Culture*. Bloomington: Indiana University Press.

Geertz, Clifford
1973 *The Interpretation of Cultures*. New York: Basic Books.
1983 Blurred Genres: the Refiguration of Social Thought. In: [s.n.], *Local Knowledge: Further Essays in Interpretive Anthropology*. New York: Basic Books, 19–35.

Hufford, Marry
1995 Context. *The Journal of American Folklore* 108 (403): 528–549.

Kapchan, Deborah A.
1995 Performance. *The Journal of American Folklore* 108 (430): 479–508.

Kozorog, Miha
2011 Festivali, festivalizacija, in festivalski kraji. http://www.sigic.si/odzven/festivali-festivalizacija-in-festivalski-kraji (accessed 6 May 2012).

Kumer, Zmaga
1978 Godčevstvo in sodobni instrumentalni ansambli na Slovenskem. In: Baš, Angelos, and Slavko Kremenšek (eds.), *Pogledi na etnologijo*. Ljubljana: Partizanska knjiga, 365–378.
1996 *Vloga, zgradba, slog slovenske ljudske pesmi*. Ljubljana: Znanstvenoraziskovalni center SAZU.

Lakoff, George, and Mark Johnson
1980 *Metaphors We Live by*. Chicago: University of Chicago.

Lévi-Strauss, Claude

1955 The Structural Study of Myth. *The Journal of American Folklore* 68 (270): 428–444.

1981 Structuralism and Myth. *The Kenyon Review* 3 (2): 64–88.

Qureshi, Regula Burckhardt

1987 Musical sound and Contextual Input: A Performance Model for Musical Analysis. *Ethnomusicology* 31 (1): 56–86.

Slobin, Mark

2000 *Subcultural Sounds: Micromusics of the West*. New England, Hanover and London: Wesleyan University Press.

Stokes, Martin

2004 Music and the Global Order. *Annual Review of Anthropology* 33: 47–72.

Šivic, Urša

2007 Vpliv institucionalnih meril na spreminjanje ljudskega petja. *Traditiones* 36 (2): 27–41.

Trstenjak, Anton

1991 *Misli o slovenskem človeku / Thoughts about Slovenian person*. Ljubljana: Založništvo slovenske knjige.

Turner, Victor

1982 *From Ritual to Theater: The Human Seriousness of Play*. New York: PAJ Publications.

1987 *The Anthropology of Performance*. New York: PAJ Publications.

1995 *The Ritual Process: Structure and Anti-Structure*. New York: Aldine De Gruyter.

Verbuč, David

2008 *Gorših ljudi na svetu ni: Terenski posnetki ljudskih pesmi iz Zgornje Savinjske doline / There are no finer people in the world: Field recordings of folk songs from the Upper Savinja Valley*. Mozirje: Osrednja knjižnica, Ljubljana: Glasbenonarodopisni inštitut ZRC SAZU, Ljubljana: Društvo za raziskovanje popularne glasbe. (CD)

2009a Accordions, merry-making, and 'tenacity' of tradition in Northern Slovenian instrumental folk music. Unpublished paper.

2009b Contemporary musical peasant traditions in Primož, Slovenia, and the notion of 'national heritage'. In: Jurková, Zuzana, and Lee Bodgood (eds.), *Voices of the Weak: Music and Minorities*. Praha: NGO Slovo 21: Faculty of Humanities of Charles University. (Accessible also through http://musicandminorities.googlepages.com/VerbucDavid_VitalContemporaryPeasant.pdf.)

Žižek, Slavoj
2003 Homo sacer as the object of the discourse of the university. http://www.lacan.com/hsacer.htm (accessed 20 February 2012).

Urša Šivic

SERBIAN BRASS BANDS IN SLOVENIA AS AN EXAMPLE OF "OUR" AND "THEIR" MUSIC

ABSTRACT

The popularity of foreign music and the adoption, imitation and adaptation of such music is a constant element in today's music scene, including this topic—the popularity and performance (imitation) of Balkan brass band music among Slovenian musicians. This article covers three different factors in more detail: a description of Slovenian Balkan brass band groups, events that are reminiscent of the "original" Balkan brass band festival in Guča (Serbia), and the competition of small instrumental groups in Dravograd (Slovenia) as the Slovenian pre-selection for the foreign, international group-competition at the Guča festival.

Key words: musical acculturation, Balkan brass bands, Yugonostalgia, festival Guča (Serbia), competition in Dravograd (Slovenia)

INTRODUCTION

In our every day life we use foreign contents on different levels: e.g. artistic, culinary, linguistic. However, culture and music also have a special position in the differentiation between what is termed "ours" and what is "foreign." In Slovenia some dishes from the countries of the former Socialist Federal Republic of Yugoslavia, like *čevapčići* (small kebabs), *pljeskavica* (burgers) and *ražnjići* (a type of shish-kebab) have become common at parties and picnics and are very much accepted as "ours," while music from these same regions has a different position and is often accepted as "theirs." Music can also very quickly become problematic, in the sense of national or aesthetic connotations.

In modern Slovenian colloquial speech the expression "Balkan" usually refers the countries of former Yugoslavia. Slovenia, being farthest to the north, with historical and cultural characteristics that are connected to the Austrian-Hungarian and Alpine area, has always been treated as "the least Balkan" of the countries. While someone would say that Slovenia is the farthest north eastern Balkan state, another would say that Slovenia is not a Balkan country at all. Geographically most of the Slovenian territory belongs to the Alpine region while in the north-west it stretches into the Mediterranean and in the north-east into the Pannonian regions. Besides the influences of other neighbouring countries and regions the greater part of Slovenian music belongs to the Alpine region, which is defined by: leaping melodies; a syllabic relation between melody and lyrics; 2/4 and 3/4 meters; the polka and the waltz that originate from traditional dances and from the 1950's onwards have represented two forms of the Slovenian modern national music—the pop-folk music genre (*narodno-zabavna glasba*). This genre originated as partly functional and partly structural in traditional music and is very much present in the media (on the national and also commercial radio and TV stations and is popular at private and public social events such as *veselica* events (a village dance usually organised by the local volunteer fire department), dances, meetings or personal anniversaries; see more Knific 2005).

Historically Slovenians were strongly influenced by the region of the Habsburgs, which defines them with middle European identity, and later, after 1918, Slovenia formed part of the South Slavs state. The latter part of history strongly connected Slovenians with Balkan culture. During this period the presence of the Balkans existed subconsciously, no matter what the intensity of the individual, community or generational contacts was. Due to historical predisposition we cannot explain the popularity of Balkan music in Slovenia in the same way as the popularity of some other foreign music, for example Latin music.

After Slovenia became independent in 1991 in a relatively short period, the conflicts that accompanied the disintegration of Yugoslavia in that same year did not negatively influence the perception of Yugoslav cultures from the historical-political point of view. There certainly are individual negative reactions and perceptions of the Serbian culture having in mind that

Serbia was an aggressor in the 1991 war for Slovenian independence. Still, these cannot compare to the conflicting, negative attitudes present in the Serbian-Croatian relationship. However as a young European Union member Slovenia has tended to move towards the European Union and is trying to shake off the historical and political ties with the Balkans.

On the other hand, to satisfy their need for hedonism, a lot of Slovenians like to search for the opposites to their "square" Alpine music, expressed in the 2/4 and 3/4 meter for the polka and the waltz respectively. In the emotionally contrasting Balkan music, the accompanying factors are quite contrary, such as a different atmosphere, dancing, food and an overall sense of positive chaos. Therefore, nostalgia for a certain historical period called Yugonostalgia and Titonostalgia (Velikonja 2008) and visiting Balkan countries, have become a popular trend in Slovenia. This is the topic that the present article deals with and especially with the popularity, adaptations and imitations of Balkan brass band music following the question: does the understanding of the discussed topic need the model of world music in the sense of broader music phenomenon or it is more appropriate to use the model of the intertwining of world music and Yugonostalgia which explains emotional ties linked to the specific historical and political conditions.

THE POPULARITY OF BALKAN MUSIC IN SLOVENIA

The popularity of Balkan music is not limited to Slovenia. It is also present in Europe and beyond and can be perceived as part of the events going on within the broader concept of world music or as a new phenomenon of the popularity of music, its hybrid form and the new musical activity (Kovačič 2009: 142–143). In Slovenia this popularity is reflected in two ways: (1) in the popularity of individual Balkan music styles and their performers (e.g. Dalmatian multipart singing, Balkan brass band music, Serbian turbo folk, Croatian, Serbian and other pop music), and (2) in Balkan musical influences in Slovenian music. One of those influences is the Balkan brass band music performed by Slovenian musicians, this also being the subject of this paper. I am using two expressions in the text: (1) (Slovenian) Balkan brass bands; this denotes those Slovenian brass bands which imitate "the original" Balkan groups in their style, behaviour and repertoire;[1] (2) ("original") Balkan brass bands (*trubači* (in Serbian), *bra(s)sovci* (in colloquial Slovenian), brass band musicians), which serve as the source for imitation by the Slovenian groups. In Slovenia the Serbian expression *trubači* represents music performed mostly by Serbian and Roma brass bands but also used for Slovenian performers and has both negative and positive connotations.

Slovenians use the general term Balkan music to refer to numerous larger and smaller occurrences of such music. On one hand Balkanisation refers to the popularity of the Croatian,[2] Serbian, Macedonian, Montenegrin and Bosnian performers of traditional, pop, rock, neo-folk and turbo-folk music. This music reaches the audience via the usual media (radio, television, internet) and because of the geographic vicinity to a large extent also through live performances. On the other hand Balkanization can also mean the influence of different Balkan music genres on Slovenian music: for example the use of the typical ornamentation of melodic lines in pop music, the use of specific instruments like tambours and brass instruments as well as the imitation of specific music genres. E.g. Robert Pešut - Magnifico is the central figure of this musical hybrid. Besides classic rock instruments he also uses brass instruments (tenor saxophone, trumpet and tuba) in the manner of Balkan brass bands. He has included an "original" Balkan brass band performer—Roma saxophonist Ferus Mustafov—in his newest project *Magnification* (2010). Some performers like Werner Brozović, Brigita

1 Although this is a regionally broader musical occurrence so the brass bands' tradition discussed in this paper includes Serbian, Romanian, Roma ... musical traditions I use the expression Balkan brass bands or the Serbian word *trubači*, usually used in Slovenia.

2 Unlike Serbian music, Croatian tamboura music and the Dalmatian multipart singing (*klapsko pjevanje*)—usually combined—, are seen by Slovenians as two cliché examples of traditional Croatian music, and have been positively accepted in Slovenia, without any negative "anti-Yugoslav," "anti-Balkan" associations. Performances of this music mean especially nostalgic evocation of the Mediterranean space and a contrast and compensation for their own national music (cf. Šivic 2009).

Šuler, Saša Lendero, Natalija Kolšek use tambouras accompaniment as an evocation of Croatian, primarily Dalmatian music tradition.

The music I am presenting in this paper is for Slovenians the prototype of the "typical" Balkan (especially traditional Serbian) music genre. Despite the diversity of Balkan traditional music styles, the brass band music as just one of them has become dominant and characteristic in the larger community. The popularity of Balkan brass band music in Slovenia was affected by Emir Kusturica's movies and the music of Goran Bregović,[3] Balkan brass band's performances at festivals, concerts, and by visiting the festival of brass band music in Guča in Serbia (discussed about later). Other occasions where this music is played in Slovenia are: appearances in restaurants with Serbian cuisine, picnics, marches through the towns, and, most recently, playing at tables in restaurants and other establishments.

Besides all that it is necessary to mention the duration of time that is necessary for a revival of music with historical and political connotations, as is happening now in Slovenia with Balkan music. Here the imitation of Balkan brass band music became more noticeably popular approximately ten years after the disintegration of Yugoslavia. In recent times we can notice more and more information that confirms the "legitimization" of Balkan or "Yugoslav music." Although "Yugoslav music" is not an appropriate term, as in the case of the Federal Republic of Yugoslavia we cannot talk about Yugoslav but Slovenian, Croatian, Serbian ... culture (language, music, art etc.), today expressions and abbreviations like "YU," "ex-YU," "ex-Yugo" are daily used. These have been given a broader contextual meaning, as a notion which on a higher level, above the political connotation, combines musical (and other) activities of the entire area of the former Yugoslav republics.[4]

3 Criticism of Goran Bregović's music in films by Emir Kusturica relates primarily to the fact that by incorporating elements of traditional Balkan music he creates "idealised sounds of other exotic nations with whom westerners are not very familiar" (Dumnic 2008: 125).

4 E.g. Radio Aktual advertised its program with these words: "There you can definitely hear the most Ex-Yugo music" (advertising billboard, 2009). In Cinema Šiška (*Kino Šiška*) in Ljubljana, which is now renovated and used for alternative cultural venues,

SLOVENIAN BALKAN BRASS BANDS

The phenomenon of Slovenian Balkan brass bands—i.e. brass bands imitating Balkan brass band music—is fairly new in Slovenia. Since Slovenian brass orchestras in a western European manner have been spread as one of the strongest amateur and professional music activities since the 19th century it is natural that Balkan brass band music is performed by musicians coming from those instrumental formations.

Today there are approximately eight brass bands in Slovenia who combine playing Balkan brass band music with other repertoire.[5] Their beginnings go back to the late 1990's, while most groups have formed only since 2000. The groups are most often formed out of smaller groups which played at private parties or as smaller sections of large brass bands. Some of these groups were formed spontaneously and others were formed from larger, more organised groups, both with the intention of playing acoustically, independent from the percussions or sounding and moving freely among the audience while playing: "The purpose in the final was to form a brass band and to play music live without the help of keyboards and midi format files."[6] The groups identify themselves differently within the concept of the Balkan brass band: some only so much as their Balkan brass band

---

there is a series of concerts of alternative music from former Yugoslav countries with the title *Yu Go* (*Kino Šiška* s.a.).

5 *Kar češ Brass Band* from Cerkno (founded in 1998); *Dej še'n litro* from Divača (founded in 1999); *Brass band Radlje* from Radlje ob Dravi (founded in 2005); *D'Palinka band* from Krško (founded in 2005); *Fešta band* from Velenje (founded in 2006); *Strizzy* from Ljubljana (founded in 2006); *Donald Trumpet brass band* from Divača (founded in 2006); *Balkan Boys* from Ljubljana (founded in 2009). The names of the groups are mostly spontaneous and funny or follow the colloquial versions of spelling: e.g. *Kar češ Brass Band*—"kar češ" in this context means "anything you like," because the band can play anything; *Dej še'n litro*—give us another litre of wine; *Fešta band*—party band; *D'Palinka band*—the band members took the name from the well known Hungarian brandy *palinka*, as they believed that, in the same way as the drink, they "burn" on stage (a pun on the Slovenian word *zažgati*, meaning burn, which in Slovenian denotes a powerful performance); Janko Uršič, personal communication with Urša Šivic, 4 April 2012.

6 Janko Uršič, personal communication with Urša Šivic, 4 April 2012.

hits make up part of their repertoire, others try to define themselves as a "original" musicians, e.g. *Fešta band* also known as *Velenjski trubači* (The Velenje Balkan Brass Band).

Slovenian Balkan brass bands perform on very diverse occasions: at concerts, on the streets and at public festivities. Balkan brass band music represents the primary part of their repertoire or a part of their extended repertoire. When they appear in the function of Balkan brass bands they appear mostly at festivals and concerts. This means that on such occasions Balkan brass band's standard hits represent the core repertoire. In cases of more spontaneous events like public festivities those bands often replace local musicians and by performing different genres they play the role of the traditional musician, who is able to adapt the heterogeneous repertoire to the wishes of their audience: "They also play different music (Slovenian, rock) and not only Balkan brass bands' hits, in this way they can meet the broad needs for music at village dances." (*Fešta band* s.a.) These groups are only partly recognised for playing Balkan brass band music as their repertoire includes also Slovenian pop-folk music and different genres of Slovenian and foreign popular music. E.g. *Kar češ Brass Band* plays Slovenian pop-folk music, traditional Balkan and Roma music, adaptations of Metallica hits, as well as New Orleans music (*Kar češ* … 2009). *D'Palinka band* plays "Slovenian popular songs, songs popular in the times of the Socialist Federal Republic of Yugoslavia and evergreens from all around the world" (*D'Palinka Band* s.a.). *Fešta band* from Velenje divides their repertoire in three parts: (1) "Our pieces—a nostalgia of typical traditional songs and some more modern examples of popular music" ("Marsch na Drino," "Užiko kolo," "Djurdjev dan," "Hava nagila," "Kalašnikov," "Mesečina," "Odpisani Jugoslavija," "Računajte na nas," "Lipe cvatu," "Za Beograd," "Gas Gas," "U planine," "Lane moje," "Intro," "Bubamara," "Čaje Šukarije" …), (2) "Slovenian songs"—mostly pop-folk hits and (3) "Rock'n'roll" (*Fešta band* s.a.). Unlike some other groups which started off with a broad repertoire, *Fešta band* started with the Balkan music, i.e. "southern"[7] music: "After some rather good band practice, when we learnt the music really well,

7 The term "southern" (*južen*) in Slovenia is the (mostly negative) expression for anything associated with former Yugoslav region.

we found that we started to enjoy playing the "southern" pieces more and more as they are very melodic. Also, there isn't a party without these pieces. After only several performances we decided to broaden our repertoire" (*Fešta band* s.a.).

Slovenian Balkan brass bands also tend to follow the "original" Balkan brass bands in their choice of instruments. Therefore their "classic" instruments include a trumpet, a trombone, a saxophone (alto and tenor), bass tube, accordion (diatonic or chromatic), guitar, drums (bass drum, darabuka, snare drum). The vocals, which can also accompany the instruments, do not have a central role and are not often used. The musicians come from already existing brass bands, they are often professional classically trained musicians active in other genres, mostly playing classical music (classical brass band music or classical orchestra music) and jazz.

THE IMPORTANCE OF THE GUČA FESTIVAL (SERBIA) IN SLOVENIA

The Balkan brass band festival in Guča (*Sabor trubača Guča*), started in 1961, was originally a Serbian national competition of small brass bands. Later foreign, non-Serbian groups joined the festival informally. The festival is visited by a large number of people, in 2002 a record 300,000 visitors attended the event (*Guča madness* … s.a.). Lately it has become very popular among foreigners from different countries (including Slovenia), who come for the music, food and fun. As mentioned before, the Guča festival in Serbia is of great importance for Slovenians. According to the interviewee, a tourist guide at the agency which organises visits of the Guča event, the festival popularity among the Slovenians—at least those who travel through the agencies—reached its peak in 2005.[8] One aspect of the festival's popularity can be seen not only in the number of Slovenian visitors, but also in the importance of the appearance of a Slovenian Balkan brass band at the event. The first Slovenian band which appeared—then

8 Saša Fras, personal communication with Mojca Kovačič and Urša Šivic, 19 February 2008.

out of the competition—at the Guča festival was a group *Dej še'n litro*. Appearing at Guča festival is an honour for the Slovenian bands and represents an important affirmation for musicians.

In the last years an interesting turnaround has taken place, i.e. the popularity of events in Slovenia which echo the Guča festival. These are not 24 hour events with non-stop performances as in Guča; however, they do evoke the Guča festival in the name and the concept. The latter combines the idea of the Balkan (predominantly) brass band music and other, broader aspects (culinary, hedonistic …) of Guča. Promotion and responses to such events often aim for the emotive experience of the "original" festival in Guča by choosing words such as: "Do you wish to experience the real Guča atmosphere? 27th and 28th August 2012, there will be an international ethno festival Guča after Guča at the Prečna near Novo mesto airport" (*Koncert: Guča po Guči* 2010). Or: "Those who missed the legendary Guča festival had an opportunity to experience some of the spirit of that festival this Friday at the Prečna near Novo mesto airport" (*Guča po Guči* 2010). Prečna near Novo mesto thus organises the festival called *Guča po Guči* (Guča after Guča), while the popularity of music or the organisation of such events has spread and has reached all the way to the Slovenian community in Italy. Since 2009 an event called *Guča na Krasu/Guča sul Carso* (Guča in Karst) has been organised in Briščiki near Trieste. A part of the event takes place in summer while in winter the event is called *Guča na Krasu winter edition* (Guča in Karst winter edition). The event brings together the "original" Balkan brass bands and various bands that play Balkan brass band music or any more or less similar Balkan music.[9] Guča is also present in the private circles. E.g. in 2007 the group *Dej še'n litro* organised a private party with typical "Balkan" food and music, which they called the Guča after party, for their friends and those who accompanied the band at Guča festival.

9 Bands appearing at Guča po Guči in 2010 (*Festival Guča po Guči* 2010) and bands appearing at Guča na Krasu in 2011 (*Glasba brez meja* 2011).

THE DRAVOGRAD COMPETITION (SLOVENIA)

Since 2007 an event called *Srečanje malih inštrumentalnih skupin* (the Meeting of Small Instrumental Groups) has been taking place in Dravograd, which further enforces the importance of the Guča festival in Slovenia. It includes a national competition which is also a pre-selection of non-Serbian groups for the foreign bands' competition at Guča. The name of the event *Zlata trobenta Dravograda* (The Golden Trumpet of Dravograd) is taken from a Serbian event *Zlatna truba Balkana* (The Golden Trumpet of the Balkans). The event in Dravograd started in 2007 and already in 2008 it had turned into a competition. The choice of Dravograd is not a coincidence. Dravograd and Lučani are twin cities and Guča is part of the Lučani area. The exchanges between the two republics and cities were common in the times of Socialist Federal Republic of Yugoslavia. After the disintegration of Yugoslavia the contacts were cut. However, in 2005 they were re-established, first in the field of sports and later in culture. Thus an idea developed to host *mala Guča* (small Guča) in Dravograd, which would partly serve as the promotion for the Guča festival. In addition, the organisers of the Guča festival wanted to have a pre-selection of the Slovenian bands for their foreign, non-Serbian part of the competition, which first took place in 2010. Before that the non-Serbian bands had appeared in the non-competitive part of the programme.[10] At the beginning, there were some negative reactions—expressed mainly by the older generation of Dravograd inhabitants—to the organisation of the event in Dravograd as they regarded it as co-operation with Serbia, an aggressor in the 1991 war for Slovenian independence. It is interesting to note that the co-operation on the sports field was not problematic, not even from the beginning. Only when the co-operation moved into culture the first negative reactions appeared.[11]

All small instrumental groups from Slovenia as well as from Slovenian communities abroad can enter the competition (regardless of their choice

10 In the future Dravograd may host even a larger regional, international competition for Slovenia, Austria, Slovakia ...

11 Robert Preglau, personal communication with Urša Šivic, 2 July 2011.

of instruments[12]), the maximum number of the people in the band being twelve. The basic idea of the event is co-operation of unusual and original groups of musicians regardless of their musical genre (jazz, classical music, rock, pop-folk …). Unusual refers to those groups whose original roster of instruments separates them from the classic music groups (*Razpis* 2012). The organisers choose "up to 15 groups" (*Razpis* ... 2011), although the competition itself is not yet so well-established as to attract more than a few groups. Each group performs three competition compositions and two compositions of their own choice for the free programme. The competitive part has to include one original or adapted Slovenian and Serbian folk song respectively. The third composition is chosen by the group. All the music has to be performed instrumentally only.[13]

In Dravograd the competing bands consider the prize for "the best brass group" to be more important than any other achievement, including the overall prize. The group who wins this title becomes the Slovenian representative at the International Competition of the Brass Bands in Guča, first organised in 2010.[14] Unlike their performance in Dravograd, the foreign groups appearing at the Guča festival play their own and not Serbian music. They are expected to present their own national music tradition and not an imitation of the "Balkan" music, which is (originally and well) played by their local bands. By diversifying the repertoire and the bands from the "Balkan" to "non-Balkan," the international competition reflects its musical globalisation and ultimately the understanding of this event as music of the world phenomenon.

12 Although different instruments are welcome, the focus is on the brass instruments (ibid.).

13 Ibid.

14 In addition to this prize (first awarded in 2012) the jury in Dravograd also awards a prize for "the best first trumpet (the best trumpet player will be awarded a trumpet)" and a prize for "the most authentic adaptation of a Slovenian composition" (*Razpis* 2012). The competition is assessed by an international jury of three, which includes two Slovenian members and one Serbian member.

CONCLUSION

Previously I observed the popularity of the Dalmatian multipart (*klapa*) singing in Slovenia and I was able to find correlations between this musical phenomenon and Balkan brass band music in Slovenia (Šivic 2009). It is possible to regard those two music genres as imitative musical phenomenon, as in both cases the primary interest of the musicians is to get as close to the original of the music they are playing/singing. In the case of Slovenian Balkan brass band music this does not include only the use of instruments, the repertoire and the imitation of style but also the imitation of behaviour on stage, unusual for Slovenians: for example, musicians thrust their trumpets in the air, use dance moves, play while moving among the audience, stick bank notes on the foreheads of the trumpet players.[15]

The imitated music mostly means an ideal for Slovenian brass musicians; their musical interpretation is not a projection of their own authorship of the music they adopt, but an original in itself. Their musical result is a revival, not a transformation. Despite the efforts to be as close to the "original," imitated music as possible, Slovenian musicians are aware of the abilities of the "original" musicians. Due to cultural predispositions they cannot achieve that ability. These are words of the musicians I interviewed: "As for the technique, they [the Serbs and the Romani] are better, they ornament one tone much more while we play more exactly, from tone to tone ... When we were in Guča at the brass band festival it was interesting because we were told that the music we play is still the same ['original'] but one can feel it is played differently. One can still hear that we are Slovenians. No matter how hard we try, we cannot hide that."[16]

The use and popularity of Balkan brass band music in Slovenia is complex, therefore, to understand it we need different explanations. The concept of world music is certainly useful where this is just one type of music with

15 For the sake of an attractive performance the musicians themselves often gesture in this way more often than this is done by members of the audience, as is the habit with the "real" Balkan brass musicians and their local public.

16 Rok Nemanič, Bojan Vovk and Bojan Krajšek, personal communication with Mojca Kovačič and Urša Šivic, 13 October 2007.

a strong exotic connotation. Also Slovenia is not the only country where Balkan brass band music has been highly popular and trendy in recent times. This is a broader phenomenon (i.e. Balkan beat phenomenon). I have already mentioned the concept of traditional musicians, which can explain the connection between the authorship of musical expression and the adaptation of the repertoire because of the audience.

However, a concept typical for Slovenia is that of Yugonostalgia (Velikonja 2008). The nostalgia for the former state appears in different forms in all the newly formed states that were former members of the Yugoslav federation. The usage of this concept is appropriate because the historical evocation makes the emotional background of the Balkan brass band music in its symbolic discourse different to what it would be in case of any other adopted music. Here it is not important to what extent the individuals, communities or generations in Slovenia were part of life in the mostly Balkan Yugoslav federation, because today no generation in Slovenia can be indifferent to the music coming from the former Yugoslav republics. The response to this music can be positive or negative. Balkan brass band music excites with its specific musical expression. Besides that it evokes different emotional activities related to historical and political memory. As at all levels of Yugonostalgia it also means romanticizing and yearning for the past joint (Yugoslav) identity, social security and for everything expressed by the Yugoslav idea of "fraternity and unity."

Although the poetics of Slovenian traditional music and of the Balkan brass band music are different and we could recognize the Balkan brass band music as "theirs," we can say that, from the perspective of the fans, Balkan brass band music is also partly "ours." The question is what is "ours." If we observe the situation, we can say that the audiences of Balkan brass band music in Slovenia are not generations who fully experienced Yugoslavia and could experience this music nostalgically. The audiences are young people who have just caught the final stage of the Yugoslav federation or were even born after its disintegration. Also Slovenian performers of Balkan brass band music did not grow up with this music. They entered it anew. Some groups even started by playing Slovenian or foreign pop music and turned to Balkan brass band music later. Slovenian researcher of the Titoist nostalgia Mitja Velikonja refers to the nostalgia for what has not been immediately experienced but maintains the emotions and the narrative credibility of a personally experienced content as neostalgia (Velikonja 2008).

The popularity of Balkan brass band music in Slovenia is a similarly adopted projection. However we need to mention the explanation that for the young people who listen to Balkan brass band music it is a part of the contemporary popular culture and image. Also, this music was not what their parents listened to, so it is useful as a tool for rebellion as well. It is very true that Balkan brass band music is listened to by the youngsters to increase the generation gap (Stanković 2002: 233). The music events inspired by the Guča festival or the Balkan brass band music show that Yugo-nostalgia is not a good enough argument to understand it. It needs to be seen also in the context of the new musical (and broader cultural) movement, which does not only rely on the past, but represents a new, active participation in the field of music (Velikonja 2002: 200).

Popular music from ex-Yugoslav republics certainly emotionally evokes the opposite response to the message of Slovenian national music, traditional or modern. Serbian brass band music compensates for the Slovenian polka and waltz, the accordion being the national instrument and the isorhythmical sequence of the "square," "jumping" music. Balkan brass band music evokes the following positive connotations: slow, carefree life, great parties, warm, openhearted people, positive chaos, good food. The music has a special rhythm and meter (irregular meter, such as 5/8, 7/8 ...), ornamented melodies, a specific range of instruments, and specific behaviour, for example, the musicians climb up onto the tables and therefore have better contact with their public. Slovenians (musicians and the audience) can find the sum of these components at the Guča festival. Most Slovenians attending this festival don't have any negative impressions and besides the music they favour other factors as well. "Guča is well known for being the greatest party in the Balkans. There is the cuisine, roasted piglet, lacking hygiene. If everything was European 'tidy, clean,' I would not have gone to Guča. This has to be the Balkans: *Zastava 101* and *Yugo* cars, horses, pigs on the roads ... and besides all that there has to be the music. This is a total experience."[17]

If the nostalgia is not a story about what we once were but about what we have never been, we can follow the analogy and say that if our national music tells us what we are, the adopted music tells us what we are not. Balkan brass band music to most of its fans represents a shortcut to life which cannot be experienced in Alpine Slovenia. Also in view of the capitalist society of our time Balkan brass band music represents the preference of more than just a former political organization. Slovenians perceive Balkan brass band music as an "authentic," traditional music expression (e.g. of Serbian, Roma or wider region) and its popularity could be understood as adaptations that are free and not trapped in the folklore in the sense of music creativity. On the other hand those transformations are emotionally trapped and determined—especially for its music characteristics, political and historical ties.

17 Rok Nemanič, Bojan Vovk and Bojan Krajšek, personal communication with Mojca Kovačič and Urša Šivic, 13 October 2007.

REFERENCES

D'Palinka Band
s.a. http://www.myspace.com/dpalinkaband (accessed 1 June 2012).

Dumnic, Marija
2008 Dance in Cinema Movies of Emir Kusturica. In: Stoykova Serafimovska, Velika (ed.), *First symposium of ICTM Study group for music and dance in Southeastern Europe, 4–8 September 2008, Struga, R. Macedonia.* Skopje: Macedonian Composers's Association – SOKOM, 123–135.

Festival Guča po Guči
2010 //www.eventim.si/si/vstopnice/guca-po-guci-novo-mesto-sportno-letalisce-precna-77916/event.html (accessed 12 June 2012).

Fešta band
s.a. http://festa-band.com/zgodovina (accessed 12 June 2012).

Glasba brez meja
2011 http://www.glasbabrezmeja.com/ (accessed 12 June 2012).

Guča madness ...
s.a. http://www.guca.rs/eng/strana.php?str=history2 (accessed 1 June 2012).

Guča po Guči
2010 http://www.lokalno.si/2010/08/29/56896/aktualno/foto_guca_po_guci/ (accessed 12 June 2012).

Kar češ ...
2009 *Kar Češ Brass Band z gosti / 10. obletnica delovanja.* http://webcache.googleusercontent.com/search?q=cache:FAY24NAMCUcJ:www.jazzcerkno.si/skupine/kcbb.php+&cd=3&hl=sl&ct=clnk&gl=si (accessed 14 February 2012).

Kino Šiška
s.a. http://www.kinosiska.si/ (accessed 11 November 2011).

Koncert: Guča po Guči
2010 http://www.genspot.com/dogodek-14483/guca-po-guci.aspx (accessed 12 June 2012).

Knific, Bojan
2005 Slovenija, od kod lepote tvoje ... Narodno-zabavna glasba kot sooblikovalka sodobne slovenske popularne kulture. *Glasnik Slovenskega etnološkega društva* 45 (1/2): 73–77.

Kovačič, Mojca
2009 The music of the other or the music of ours. Balkan music among Slovenians. In: Stoykova Serafimovska, Velika (ed.), *First symposium of ICTM Study group for music and dance in Southeastern Europe, 4-8 september 2008, Struga, R. Macedonia.* Skopje: Macedonian Composers's Association – SOKOM, 137–144.

Razpis ...
2011 *Razpis. Srečanje malih inštrumentalnih skupin – državno predtekmovanje za Gučo* 2011. OI JSKD, Dravograd.

Razpis
2012 https://www.jskd.si/glasba/instrumentalna/prireditve_instrumentalna/druge/predtekmovanje_guca_12.htm (accessed, 15 June 2012).

Stanković, Peter
2002 Uporabe 'Balkana.' Rock in nacionalizem v Sloveniji v devetdesetih letih. *Teorija in praksa* 39 (2): 220–238.

Šivic, Urša
2009 Dalmatinsko klapsko pjevanje u Sloveniji. *Narodna umjetnost* 46 (32): 95–110.

Velikonja, Mitja
2002 'Balkan culture' in Slovenia after 1991. In: Törnquist-Plewa, Barbara and Sanimir Resic (ed.), *The Balkan in Focus – Cultural Boundaries in Europe.* Lund: Nordic Academic Press, 189–207.

2008 *Titostalgija. Študija nostalgije po Josipu Brozu.* Ljubljana: Mirovni inštitut.

Liz Mellish and Nick Green

TRADITIONAL FOLK DANCE PERFORMANCE IN THE 21st CENTURY: ROMANIAN *CĂLUŞ* VERSUS ENGLISH MORRIS: REVIVALIST VERSUS EX-COMMUNIST?

ABSTRACT

In this paper, the authors consider ways the dilemma "what to do about folklore?" is resolved in contemporary performances of the Romanian *căluş* and English morris. They focus their discussions around three questions: "what is the state of the performance today?", "how are these dance forms viewed by locals and as part of their nations' culture?" and "where is this going or likely to go in the future?" They conclude that, two different approaches have been taken due to factors specific to the original location of the folklore.

Key words: *căluş*, morris, folk-performance, tradition, revival

INTRODUCTION

Since the late 19th century, when rural ways of life began to disappear, a variety of approaches have been undertaken to record, preserve and even revive rural folklore in different parts of the world. Many of these approaches have led to new or adapted forms of the original material which most "traditionalists" regard as "folklorism." In this paper, the authors will consider the ways that this dilemma has been resolved in two specific places, Romania and England, in connection with the theme of this book "trapped in folklore" by focussing their discussions around two specific traditions, the Romanian *căluş* and English morris. Research into rural traditions, dance and song started in both countries around the same time. However, after 1948 Romania followed the Soviet model of folklore performance, with an abundance of professional and amateur folk ensembles and regular national competitions to stimulate folklore production, whilst in England folk dance has remained as a minority interest, despite revivals occurring in the 1960s and 1970s, and the term "folk" is often seen as having a rural uncultured image.

The aim of this article is to make comparisons between these two traditions by focussing discussion towards three specific questions: "what is the state of the performance today?", "how are these dance forms viewed by locals and as part of their nations' culture?" and "where is this going or likely to go in the future?" We address these questions from the perspective of a connection to the community, taking a hypothesis that the state of performance of the folklore is related to the wider community's perception of the folklore, and that the performers of these dances do this for recreation as part of their social life.

ROMANIAN *CĂLUŞ* VERSUS ENGLISH MORRIS

Romanian *căluş* has predominantly two forms, the *căluş* healing ritual of southern Romania (also found in the neighbouring regions of northern Bulgaria) that takes place every year at the time of *Rusalii* (Pentecost) and the *căluş*er dances of southern Transylvania and Banat which are performed as part of the new year rituals (see for example Kligman (1981) and Giurchescu (1992)). English morris is best known for the dances documented in the "Cotswold" villages in the southern Midlands of England which still continue to be danced in a few villages. However, there are similar dance practices documented in the southwest Midlands, now commonly referred to as "Border morris," in eastern England, as "Molly dances" and in Lancashire and Cheshire, in northwest England there is a different form also referred to as Morris, or "Clog morris."[1] English morris dance has been part of several 20th century folk revivals, and it was early in this revival history, by 1912, the myth that morris was a survival of ancient ritual customs had been initiated (Buckland 2002: 419). These revival morris teams are connected through three country wide associations; The Morris Ring, The Morris Federation, and Open Morris.[2]

1 England also has several hit-and-sword dancing traditions which are not connected to morris, although often included within "morris" by dance enthusiasts.

2 The websites for The Morris Ring, The Morris Federation, and Open Morris can be found at http://www.themorrisring.org/, http://www.morrisfed.org/ and http://www.open-morris.org/ (all accessed 21 January 2012).

Similarities can be seen between the older village versions of English morris and Romanian *căluş* in terms of the participants and their performance. Both have teams of men with a leader and involve dances in which the dancers perform a set of rehearsed steps and figures in unison, in some cases with the aid of a prop such as a stick. Most often the dancers wear some form of costume based on the local rural dress of white linen with coloured ribbon decoration. By setting out these points of general similarity the authors are not intending to endorse any proposal for mutual origins.[3] In this paper this comparison is intended to provide a starting point for a discussion comparing two similar dance traditions in two different folk dance constructions and the use of these within the community. An important difference between morris and *căluş* is the continued belief in the function of the *căluş* healing ritual, compared to morris being a form of dance performance predominantly for gaining money.

Both *căluş* and morris have a long history of performance, with the earliest documentary reference to English morris being in 1458 (Cutting 2005: 103), however, there are tentative references to morris in England during the preceding centuries. The earliest archival documentation, recording the performance of ritual *căluşerul* dances in front of groups of noblemen in Transylvania, is dated 1572 (Bârlea 1982: 35–36) and by the mid-19th century the *căluşer* tradition in Transylvania was being used as a means of reinforcing Romanian identity during the period of Hungarian rule (Martin 1985: 119).

HISTORY OF RESEARCH INTO RURAL TRADITIONS IN ROMANIA AND ENGLAND

Research into rural traditions, dance and song started in both countries around the same time. In England at the start of the 20th century the collector Cecil Sharp was largely responsible for the interest, documentation and revival of Cotswold morris. He collected dances and tunes, and published these in a series of books dating from 1907 (Sharp 1907, Sharp and Macilwaine 1910, Sharp and Macil-

3 This view has sometimes been part of speculative discussions in popular culture. For example see the Wikipedia pages at http://en.wikipedia.org/wiki/Morris_dance and http://en.wikipedia.org/wiki/C%C4%83lu%C5%9Fari (both accessed 21 January 2012).

waine 1911). In 1909 the morris dance was included in the Board of Education's syllabus of physical exercise (Sharp and Macilwaine 1910: 7), and in 1934 six clubs founded "The Morris Ring," which became the national association for morris men (Peck 1949: 1). In Romania, research into folk dance started around 1910 under the auspices of the Romanian Academy, and in 1921–22 the academic Romulus Vuia[4] published an article on the origins of the *căluş* (Vuia 1997 (1922)). The ritual aspects of the *căluş* tradition have been the subject of extensive scholarly works in Romanian literature (Oprisan 1969, Semuc 2009, Stancu 1997) together with discussions on the appropriation of this tradition as a national symbol during the communist regime (Giurchescu 2001: 115–117, Giurchescu 2004, Kligman 1981, Proca-Ciortea 1978) and the listing of the *căluş* tradition as UNESCO intangible heritage (Giurchescu 2009, Mellish 2006).

The first occasion when morris met *căluş* was at an international folk festival held in London in 1935. The participants at this festival included a Cotswold morris team and a *căluş* group from the southern Romanian village of Pădureţi (Howes 1935). The *căluş* dancers created a stir in London by refusing to dance until Douglas Kennedy, Chairman of the English Folk Dance and Songs Society (EFDSS), scoured London to locate fresh garlic for their ritual flag, as without this they did not consider they would have their supernatural powers (Giurchescu 2004, Mellish 2006: 5). After the Second World War the dances included in the *căluş* ritual were choreographed into dance suites which were included in performances by the wide network of folk ensembles that were established based on the Soviet model of folklore performance, and from 1976 an annual *căluş* festival was held in the town of Slatina (Giurchescu 1990: 53). At the same time the practice of the ritual *căluş* was forbidden in villages as part of the central drive for modernisation (Kligman 1981, Mellish 2006).

Despite a succession of revivals since Cecil Sharp's activities, particularly those in the 1950s, and 1970s, English morris dance has remained largely

4 Romulus Vuia (1887–1963) was the first director of the Transylvania Ethnographic Museum in Cluj. In Romania early research into folk dance was also undertaken by Niculescu-Varone (1884–1994) who travelled round villages collecting dances in the period from 1919 to 1934 (Niculescu-Varone and Gainariu-Varone, 1979), and the ethnomusicologist Constantin Brăilou (1893–1958).

a minority recreational interest for urban participants who formed a community network linked by a mutual interest, or what Turino terms as a "cultural cohort" (Turino 2008: 235). Some teams in the 1970s revival challenged the Morris Ring's conservative approach by creating new styles and forms of performance presentation and in particular the rule that limited participation only to men, by allowing women to participate in the dancing (Buckland 2006: 26). In parallel to these developments, in the Cotswolds a few village teams continued, or were revived, based on continuous dancing of their tradition within the village community.

WHAT IS THE STATE OF THE PERFORMANCE TODAY?

Căluş and morris both continue to be performed in Romania and England respectively. In Romania, the *căluş* ritual is still performed in a few villages, there are also village based groups that only perform *căluş* dances (Giurchescu 2004), and the majority of urban based folk ensembles throughout Romania include a suite of *căluş* dances in their performance repertoire. In England there is a cultural cohort network of revival morris teams that are linked through one of the three nationwide organisations, and these teams are formed from members that are often lifelong enthusiasts and continue to dance in the teams from youth to well past retirement age.

In both Romania and England, the traditional or folk dance repertoire included dances for social occasions and dances for performance only. In general the performance forms are centred on men's dances, originally performed only by all male groups, whereas the social dances are for mixed participation of men and women in couples or circle formations. In post Second World War Romania, social dance forms were arranged for performance to an audience by choreographers from folk ensembles. This transfer from social dance to performance has been far less prevalent in the English folk dance world, with only occasional attempts to choreograph social dances for performance to an audience. Thus social dances have remained as a participatory form used only at social occasions.

The Romanian dance ensembles have maintained the gender separation for the performance of dances that were originally men's dances, but the ensembles have brought the social dances to the stage for mixed gender performance. It should be noted that the ensembles also have social events at which the members participate in the social dance repertoire in their un-staged form. In the morris teams many have progressed to become mixed gender teams or have invited both men's and women's team to events, which leads to mixed gender performance of the previously male dominated performance dance.

The *căluş* tradition used to take place in villages, being performed in the street or house courtyards, with the *căluşari* going for house to house performing their ritual as required by the households. Similarly morris was performed on the street or in other available spaces, and these performance spaces have been maintained by the various revivalist movements. In Romania, performances by folk ensembles and village dance groups now usually take place on a raised platform or customised arena space which gives a different vantage point for the spectator, whereas morris is nearly always performed at the same level as the audience. This is probably in line with the cultural expectations in the two countries. In Romania, facilities such as theatre stages, open air theatres and temporary stages are readily available for events, and these provide a location that has audience areas with good viewing positions. In England the hiring of such facilities is expensive and generally beyond the finances for folk groups. Also the cultural linking of these to high arts events leads to a desire from many of the revival folk participants to separate their dancing from such an association.

The participants of the dance have changed due to the transfer of dances to the English revival teams and the Romanian ensembles. As mentioned above the Romanian *căluş* dances were originally from certain regions, hence there was once a locational limit to participants. However, it is now included in the performance repertoire of ensembles from all regions of Romania[5] and in the same way, morris from the Midlands ("Cotswold" in the south Midlands and "Border"

5 This is mostly true for the southern *căluş*, whereas the Transylvanian and Banat *căluşeri* are seldom included in folk ensemble's repertoire outside of their regions of origin.

in the west Midlands) is now danced by groups based in all regions of England. Linked to this transfer to a nationwide participation is an increase in urban participants. The revival movement in English folk dance has a significant urban base (see for example the list of Morris Ring member teams (Peck 1949)). Many of the ensembles in Romania are urban based and the participants are typically university students and graduates, although there is also a strong base of village groups whose participants are either children's or of mixed age. There is a historical difference between Romania and England in people's connections to the rural village. In England, by the early 20th century the industrial revolution had given rise to a predominately urban population, with the majority not retaining family connections to a village, whereas in Romania the increase in urbanisation took place only after the second world war and many Romanian urbanites still maintain regular contact with their family villages where elderly family members still reside.

As discussed above, the gender mix has changed; since the 1970s the revival morris teams have included, firstly women's teams and later many mixed teams, blurring the previous gender separation between performance and social dance forms, whereas Romanian ensembles usually have an equal number of male and female dancers, but only the men perform the *căluş* dances.[6] These changes in participants appear to have put the English morris revival and the Romanian ensemble membership to approximately the same basis; a mixed gender social group dancing for recreation, from countrywide locations and there is a significant membership of urbanites. In terms of the people involved, the authors suggest that the motivation for dancing and socialising in recreational traditional dance groups is the same in England and Romania. Today, morris dance takes place in the revival side and is regarded as a social activity, with a focus on an English pub and in some cases is more social than dance!

During the Romanian communist period potential choreographers attended a state organised training scheme, and more recently local training schemes have

6 In Romania we have observed a recent trend for the inclusion of women performing dressed as men both in *căluş* dance suites and during suites of couple dances where the ensemble has a lack of men.

been set up in the main cities of Romania. In Romanian ensembles, dance instruction is usually undertaken by the ensemble choreographer who in many cases gained his or her dance knowledge through their own participation as a dancer in one of the urban ensembles, but often also had a village background. Dance instructors connection with urban ensembles does lead to the dissemination of urban performance ideas into the villages setting, but this is not a new phenomenon, as Bartók noted that Romanian communities are "inclined to take over the habits of performance of urban people" (Bartók 1967: 4).

In England, morris teams and folk dance groups can be started by any keen person. These individuals are often from the social dance environment and have little trained dance experience. Through the 20th century the Morris Ring organisation was instrumental in maintaining the quality of revival teams by organising teaching workshops, however, the desire to remain as a "folk" activity in English culture perceptions could be viewed as leading to the reverse of the Romanian situation. Performance ideas that are seen as urban high culture are rejected for ideas that are perceived as "rural" by the current community of participants. In terms of attitudes to performance the two forms appear to have moved in opposite directions. Morris dates from the period of gentile, graceful male dance, yet the post 1970s developments have a tendency to depict the rural as rustic and ungraceful, but this could be part of a general trend in male dance in twentieth century England as well as a reflection on the way that rural life is viewed. In Romania the ensembles strive for the grace and control that comes with dance training, and stage presentation skill with an aim to depict the village as refined.

The choreographed version of the *căluş* dances performed by folk ensembles had certain features of the original custom removed as these were considered inappropriate during the communist period (Kligman 1977: 36), and the dance is choreographed to highlight finesse and virtuosity where "dancer's dexterity is officially acknowledged and rewarded" (Kligman 1981: 150). The participants in the Morris Ring revival teams aim to try and maintain the morris dances without making any changes in the manner of performance from the village teams in the Cotswold villages. However, after the 1970s revival, re-inventions and creations were added to the repertoire of English morris, with these more recent performances having vigorous dancing, often in diverse brightly coloured costumes, in comparison to the gentile nature of earlier Cotswold dancing. These changes may be more to do with the cultural expectations in the two countries than with debates on the "correct" preservation of folklore. A valid discussion could consider allowing performances to change to find a new purpose in the community versus allowing creativity to give life in artistic terms, but will too much artistic creativity lead to a short term fashion and not a community tradition?

HOW IS THIS VIEWED AS PART OF THE NATION'S CULTURE?

The different histories of *căluş* and morris have influenced how these two traditions have continued to be practiced, accepted and respected within their local communities. These aspects are important to the continuation or preservation of a tradition both in terms of those who perform the dances and the audience, as without acceptance, the local community is unlikely to provide an appreciative audience. A "living" tradition might be seen as one where the community of participants use their creativity to change and progress the dance into new art forms, for example some of the post 1970s English morris. However, this can also separate the "living" tradition from the local community, leaving the appreciative audience as those predominantly from within the cultural-cohort, so only a network of interested enthusiasts. We have found during our research in Romania that the local forms of music and dance are often still used in the local community, both in towns and in villages, and are given respect by the community, including those that choose not to participate. This leads to less change and creativity in the performance practices, but a continuing participation in traditional dance and music activities in the wider community. The authors would suggest that the underlying views of "rural" or village life in England and Romania can be considered as a major factor in how the *căluş* and morris tradition are viewed by the mass of the population in England and Romania.

In England, rural is often viewed as rustic and uncultured, so English morris dancing with its rural associations is often ridiculed in the British media and on television It is not seen as a cultural treasure, instead it is often considered as a social activity on the edge of the community. This leads to media comments such as,

"But we are distancing ourselves at an ever-increasing rate from our folk culture. [...] the English folk dance and song movement has been reduced to a curiosity, an anomaly, almost an object of ridicule" (*This Is Bristol* 2009).

"A lot of people have misconceptions about morris dancing. They don't know anything about it but choose to ridicule it" (McGregor 2004).

"The Morris Ring claims the stereotypical image of men prancing about in colourful costumes, waving handkerchiefs at each other with bells attached to their knees, isn't appealing to youngsters who consider the past-time an embarrassing relic" (Weatherall 2009).

Alternately, those within the newest revival movements claim that the interest in morris among youth is increasing, possibly indicating the start of another cyclical revival,

"There are more people dancing various styles of morris dancing than there has been for a long time" (McGregor 2004).

"But North morris dancers claim that just isn't true and that there is plenty of young blood coming through" (Weatherall 2009).

Unlike England, many Romanians view the village as the heart of the Romanian soul and take a pride in their rural heritage and consequently view the local music and dance, including traditional *căluş* as a national treasure that is worthy of preservation for posterity. Around 2003 an application was made to UNESCO for the recognition of the *căluş* as UNESCO intangible heritage, and this status was granted in 2005 (*UNESCO* 2005). The suite of *căluş* dances takes pride of place in staged folklore performances, and is widely conveyed this way in media. For example, the Romanian dance talent show "Dansez pentru tine" (the Romanian version of "Dancing with the Stars") which is broadcast on the national Romanian Television channel TVR2, regularly includes *căluş* dances[7] whereas similar English shows include ballroom, Latin American, contemporary, or hip hop dancing, but certainly no morris. One of these "Dansez pentru tine" performances was led by choreographer Marin Barbu and involved a mock contest between the Doina Gorjului ensemble dancers and the contestants. Marin has a family history of *căluş* and is now a star in his own right through his involvement with this television show.[8]

But why is this? Maybe the closeness of much of the Romanian population to the village holds the rural dance and music in higher respect? Maybe the various folk dance forms still form part of the lives and memories of much of the population? In England the widespread community use of such village traditions died out mostly by the 20th century, leading to morris and other folk traditions being predominantly a revivalist recreational interest for only a small part of the population.

WHERE ARE THESE TRADITIONS GOING?

The final question under consideration is where might be the future for these two dance traditions in terms of participants, community and change. In England, dancers can remain actively participating in performances for longer compared to the Romanian ensembles which tend to have a continual new entry of youth and retirement of the older members, who remain active in social events whilst occasionally dancing as "veterans." Recently in Romania there has been an increased interest in local dance, the folk ensembles currently have a strong younger membership, who in time replaces the older members in the adult groups. Many expected that after 1989 the organised ensembles and their form of dance would be rejected due to their

7 See for example http://www.protv.ro/video/dansez-pentru-tine_wilmark-reinventeaza-calusul-romanesc_2523.html (accessed 21 January 2012) or http://dansezpentrutine.protv.ro/video/12702/pagina/91/momente.html (accessed 21 January 2012).

8 An on-line video of this performance can be found at http://video.acasa.ro/muzica---videoclipuri/doina-gorjului-vs-dansez-pentru-tine-trupa-de-dans--234e3fad47fa8eabf03a.html# (accessed 21 January 2012).

close links with the communist regime. However, despite many ensembles and dance groups closing in the early 1990s due to the withdrawal of state funds and a dip in enthusiasm for folk related activities, from around 2005 renewed enthusiasm has led to an expansion of groups in all parts of Romania, and an increased interest in Romanian traditions such as *căluş* that many view as part of Romanian cultural heritage. Is it that the stronger links to rural life have led to the integration of village ensembles into the village structure (in schools and on festive occasions) often with support from the local mayor? Maybe the higher regard for folklore performance, possibly due to the image portrayed by the higher aesthetically developed urban ensembles, allows individuals to participate without ridicule? Does the stage representation of folk dances meet current expectations in performance?

So could the difficulty morris has in its image be related to the performance not meeting the expectations of the wider urban community? There is a recruitment issue with many dancers ageing, but this is not helped by the negative image of morris and the lack of connection to the community, although there are a few locations with village traditions that do regard their heritage with respect. It may be that the situation in England a century ago more closely matched that of current Romania. Although there are many more people actively participating in Romanian ensembles compared to England, and there is a much greater exposure in the community, in some areas of Romania, one can see the genre of local dancing is becoming less of a customary practice, or habit, at events, and more of a tradition, a practice continuing as a tradition that is respected.

In the Banat region of Romania we have researched the network of activities run by an array of dance teachers in collaboration with local schools and "culture houses." The sponsorship by the mayors and schools, local competitions and teaching of traditional music all helps the integration of traditional dance groups into the local community in Romania. A similar initiative through the schools can be found in the teaching of molly dancing in the Fenland region of England, in this case funded by a central source and provided by a single organisation,

"World Festivals Ltd who have been successful in obtaining funding to teach molly dancing, local story and traditions in fenlands schools since 2003. The Heritage Lottery Fund has supported three projects with an investment of nearly £300,000. Our World Festivals have so far, taught over 2000 primary school children to dance" (*Molly Dancing* 2012a).

Returning to the ideas of creativity in performance, the inventing, recreating and adapting of traditions which can be seen in some the 1970s morris revivals, several decades later is not seen as particularly representative or respected in the wider English community, or integrated into the local community. However, the creation of the so called "Border Morris" thirty years on is showing a strong following with many groups across England and so becoming a tradition in its own right. The ideas of artistic creativity are part of the direction for spreading and teaching molly dancing and other forms of English folk traditions,

"Stimulus to develop their own, often unique, style of dance, music and costume" (*Molly Dancing* 2012b).

"Aim to capture an atmosphere, style and vigour that may be associated with the ploughboys of old and of the wild, barren, dangerous nature of the landscape in which they worked" (*Molly Dancing* 2012b).

This idea of the art form of traditional dancing having an intentional creativity and positive desire to stimulate creative thinking is in contrast to Romania where there is generally less change within the current framework of the choreographic adaptation for the typical stage performance. One could argue that the existence of traditions is by definition a situation where there is less change so that the tradition has meaning to a wider range of generations in the community, although some adaptations and creations naturally become popular and set the path for the future dancing. There are some attempts to modernise and adapt to the current society, such as,

"The Demon Barbers bring traditional rapper sword dancing bang up to date by mixing it with hip hop and techno soundtrack. Now the group has just been awarded a £25,000 grant from the Arts Council to create a brand new show in the spring" (*Yorkshire Post* 2009).

Will this create a new direction and popular form for the future, or is this a creative idea that will only have temporary meaning to one generation?

CONCLUSION

This paper set out to consider to what extent two specific traditions, Romanian *căluş* and English morris have continued to be practiced as living traditions and so have not become "trapped in folklore" in a form that resisted change. It did not attempt to examine these in terms of the few villages where these traditions still exist within their communities, but in terms of the wider organisation of dance groups that continue to perform these traditions in the respective countries in the 21st century; the revival morris teams of England and the folk ensembles of Romania.

We have put forward the ideas of "respect" from the wider community and the role of "creativity" as factors that have affected the image of these dance traditions. A living "tradition" or revival has to be accepted and respected in the wider community and deliver performances that meet the community's expectations in order to continue as more than a minority interest or cultural cohort. Many Romanians view traditional *căluş* as a national treasure worthy of preservation for posterity, and as a dance which takes pride of place in staged folklore performances, whereas English morris dancing is frequently ridiculed in the British media and is considered as a social activity on the edge of the community. This difference in opinion may be related to the different histories of urbanisation in the two countries which leave the English dancers without a connection to a rural location whereas many Romanians are still closely connected to their family villages. In the Romanian case the performance has moved to stage locations, and choreographic features have been added that allow the performances to be part of the current expectations for TV media and festivals. This ease of adaption to current media presentation seems to have been aided by continued teaching and the organisational structure instigated by the initiatives of the previous socialist government, something that the predominantly socialist "folk" movement in England has not wished to pursue.

The use of "creativity" to take the dances to an artist activity by introducing changes to the format is minimal in the Romanian case. This means that performances continue to resonate with audiences from a wider background and age range. In the case of English morris attempts have been made to integrate creative versions into the current community, but it is possible that this may create a temporary "fad" which only fills a niche in contemporary culture.

The authors would conclude that the two different approaches taken have enabled the performance of these two genres to continue and that in both cases the course of action taken has been determined by external factors that are specific to the original location of the folklore.

REFERENCES

Bârlea, Ovidiu

1982 *Eseu despre Dansul Popular Românesc.* Bucureşti: Cartea Românească.

Bartók, Béla

1967 *Rumanian folk music. Volume 1: Instrumental melodies.* 1. The Hague: Martinus Nijhoff.

Buckland, Theresa Jill

2002 "Th'owd pagan dance." Ritual, Enchantment and an enduring Intellectual paradigm. *Journal for the Anthropological Study of Human Movement* 11–12 (4–1): 415–452.

2006 Dancing Northernness in a Global Context: Reflections on Embodied Concepts of Identity. The North in a Global Context. In: Lundborg, Nina (ed.), *Proceedings. 8th International NOFOD Conference.* Stockholm: NOFOD, 21–30.

Cutting, John

2005 *History and the Morris Dance – A look at morris dancing from its earliest days until 1850.* Alton: Dance Books.

Giurchescu, Anca

1990 The use of traditional symbols for recasting the present: A case study of tourism in Rumania. *Dance Studies* 14: 47–64.

1992 A Comparative Analysis between the "Căluş" of the Danube Plain and "Căluşerul" of Transylvania (Romania). *Studia Musicologica* 34 (1/2): 31–44.

2001 The power of dance and its social and political uses. *Yearbook for Traditional Music* 33: 109–121.

2004 Căluş – between ritual and national symbol. http://mainweb.hgo.se/Inst/ks.nsf/d58a35499d98cdbdc1256df100359b6b/e7f08b6b784e3534c1256f500068ca1d!OpenDocument (accessed 25 May 2008).

2009 Cum sa ajuns de la obiceiul Căluşului la tradiţia Căluşului şi la Capodopera Patrimoniului Cultural Imaterial UNESCO "Ritualul Căluşului"? Rînduială, obiceiuri şi tradi ţii sau despre ce vorbim de fapt cînd vorbim despre tradiţii? *Conferinţe de Şosea.* Bucureşti: Muzeul Ţaranului.

Howes, Frank
1935 *Journal of the English Folk Dance and Song Society.* Vol II. International Festival Number. London: EFDSS.

Kligman, Gail
1977 From the Village to the Stage: Ritual Dance and Dancers. *Balkan Arts Traditions* 111(1): 32–36.
1981 *Căluş – Symbolic Transformation in Romanian Ritual.* Chicago: University of Chicago Press.

Martin, György
1985 Peasant Dance traditions and national dance types in East – Central Europe between the 16th-19th centuries. *Ethnologia Europaea XV*, 2: 117–128.

McGregor, Mark
2004 Morris men "recruitment crisis". *BBC News (20-Nov-2004)* London: BBC. http://news.bbc.co.uk/1/hi/england/west_yorkshire/4025097.stm (accessed 30 August 2009).

Mellish, Liz
2006 The Romanian Căluş tradition and its changing symbolism as it travels from the village to the global platform. Gotland: Gotland University. http://mainweb.hgo.se/Inst/ks.nsf/0/7b686428ccfa46cbc125713f003d0109/$FILE/Mellish%202006%20Calus.pdf (accessed 25 May 2008).

Molly Dancing
2012a Molly dancing in schools. Molly Dancing. http://www.mollydancing.com/ (accessed 21 January 2012).
2012b What is molly dancing? Molly Dancing. http://www.mollydancing.com/ (accessed 21 January 2012).

Niculescu-Varone, George T, and Elena Costache Gainariu-Varone
1979 *Dicţionarul Jocurilor Populare Româneşti.* Bucharest: Editura Litera.

Oprisan, Horia Barbu
1969 *Calusarii – Studii de folclor.* Bucureşti: Editura Pentru Literatura.

Peck, Arthur
1949 Fifty Years of Morris Dancing 1899–1949. Morris Ring. http://www.themorrisring.org/50-years-booklet (accessed 21 January 2012).

Proca-Ciortea, Vera
1978 The "Căluş Custom" in Rumania – Tradition – Change – Creativity. *Dance Studies* 3: 1–43.

Semuc, Vlad-Ionut
2009 *Elemente de Geografie mitica a Romaniei Calusul.* Bucuresti: Editura Etnologica.

Sharp, Cecil. J.
1907 *The Morris Book.* London: Novello.

Sharp, Cecil J. and Herbert C. Macilwaine
1910 *The Morris Book: with a description of dances as performed by the morris-men of England.* Part 3. London: Novello.
1911 *The Morris Book: with a description of dances as performed by the morris-men of England.* Part 4. London: Novello.

Stancu, Constantin
1997 *Căluşul – antologie de studii.* Piteşti: Tiparg.

This is Bristol
2009 Only television can save morris dancing. *This is Bristol.* Bristol: Northcliffe Media. http://www.thisisbristol.co.uk/television-save-morris-dancing/story-11292278-detail/story.html (accessed 30 August 2009).

Turino, Thomas
2008 *Music as social life: the politics of participation.* Chicago: University of Chicago Press.

UNESCO
2005 Proclamation 2005: "The Căluş Ritual." http://www.unesco.org/culture/ich/index.php?lg=EN&topic=mp&cp=RO (accessed 18 September 2009).

Vuia, Romulus
1997 Originea Jocului de Căluşari. In: Stancu, Constantin (ed.), *Căluşul – antologie de studii.* Piteşti: Tiparg, 96–127.

Weatherall, Robert
2009 Young morris dancers ring the changes in North. *Sunday Sun* (11 Jan 2009) London: ncjMedia Limited. http://www.sundaysun.co.uk/news/north-east-news/2009/01/11/young-morris-dancers-ring-the-changes-in-north-79310-22665079/ (accessed 30 August 2009).

Yorkshire Post
2009 Video: When sword dancing met hip-hop. *Yorkshire Post* (14-Aug-2009) Leeds: Johnston Publishing Ltd. http://www.yorkshirepost.co.uk/news/around-yorkshire/local-stories/video_when_sword_dancing_met_hip_hop_1_2294171 (accessed 21 January 2012).

Alma Bejtullahu

OF GENDER BONDAGE: WOMEN'S MUSICAL PRACTICE AND EMPOWERMENT

ABSTRACT

This paper focuses on the musical practice of women (both instrumental and vocal music) in Kosovo and Slovenia respectively. It explores the issue of transgressing the social norms for women's music-making, the ways these norms were expanded and, eventually, how modernisation has affected women's musical practice.

Key words: female musicians, modernisation, music in Kosovo, music in Slovenia

INTRODUCTION: APPROACHING THE RESEARCH

Women's musical practices are studied from different research points of view. One of the recent approaches in studying music and gender (see Magrini 2003, Sugarman 1997) finds that complex social inter-gender relations manifested in music, are crucial in explaining the musical activities of women and their transformation during time, which is what this paper will try to address. Focusing on research areas in Kosovo and Slovenia, this paper analyzes female musicians practicing music that has had the transformation of these practices in a broader context of social changes.

The research presented tackles the research area(s) and subjects throughout the 20th century to the present, which allows comparisons to be made between practices of the past and the present. Within this temporal frame it is necessary to use non empirical methods, particularly by using secondary sources. Also, empirical methods (such as observation, gathering field information) come into effect (particularly when analyzing newer occurrences) while conducting interviews, conversations and the observation of the research subjects, by using the qualitative approach.

As far as research areas are concerned, there are several factors that need to be taken into account. In general it would be easy to distinguish two research areas—Kosovo and Slovenia—as two completely separate areas. The traditional musical practices, particularly the use of instruments, the types of melodies and musical structure have very little in common. Also the two areas are quite different from the ethnic and linguistic point of view. Culturally, Kosovo's population is regarded as more patriarchal and at the same time the heterogeneity of religions and historic influences make the issue of women quite complex[1]. Slovenia, as a (mostly) catholic country, influenced by West-European culture is regarded as an area where the status of women is regulated in a modern and diffuse way. On the other hand, there are also some common social and political turning points in the course of time that affected the musical practices of women opening the way for the modernisation of these practices. This paper analyses musical situations at several common turning points of their respective histories, such as the movement for the emancipation or the independence of the nation, gender politics in the era during the communist system and, later, the introduction of the principle of the market economy that had influence in the status of women musicians in the respective areas. While these turning points appeared to have similar effects on both societies, they occurred at different points in time and, as this paper tries to point out, there are different ways that female musical practices take the path of modernisation and urbanisation.

In the light of these situations, women as musicians had the possibility not only to transform their status and to gain power but also to contribute to the inventive processes in music. These transformations proceeded in different musical styles in accordance with time and the general taste for music; that is why this paper addresses different musical styles (rural or urban, traditional, modern, and popular) that, though structurally not bound, every time served as platform for modernizing the status of women

1 Within the relatively small area of Kosovo there are several religious influences that were layered through time; from pre-Christian beliefs, to Christianity, with Roman Catholicism, eastern (orthodox) Christianity, to Islam, which is the newest religious input.

musicians. Transformations of women's musical practices are, most of the time, specific and particular for every community. During my research on gender issues in Kosovo and Slovenia, I realized that some situations, that are a direct result of modernisation, e.g. establishing the nation, the emergence of women in professional music-making etc., have certain points in common. There are some universal features: the way women negotiate and reposition themselves as musicians is an interesting case of how women either work within the proverbial "entrapment of folklore" or follow the completely opposite path.

WOMEN[2] AND MUSIC-MAKING IN THE PAST

In some ways, the musical practices of women in the (near) past[3] are either determined by organisations in the communities that they have lived in or are blended with common (often male) musical practices. Before addressing the latter—the issue of transgression of the (usually) male repertoire to female performers—let us first look into the musical practices of the societies with clear distribution of power.

From the aspect of the "distribution of the power in a society"—men holding the power—human societies are patriarchal and patriarchy influences social organisation (Heider 1996: 142). In a society, where the powers (either economical or political etc.) are clearly divided between the genders, there also is a division between duties and responsibilities, or a division of labour (Eriksen 2009) which is often evident as a gender-divided repertoire within traditional musical practices.

Further, gender differentiation—to some extent—is also evident in the sphere of public and private, the first being available to men and the lat-

2 Fully aware of the biological implication of "sex" and, accordingly, "female" and "male" as well as the cultural implication of "gender" and "woman and man" (see Eriksen 2009), for the purposes of this paper both terms female and women within the cultural context are being used.

3 For the purposes of this research, the secondary resources used are mostly previous research from about the mid-20th century.

ter to women (Magrini 2003: 13, Sugarman 1997: 188). Nevertheless this division is not to be taken for granted: as several authors emphasise, this differentiation varies from society to society (Eriksen 2009, Koskoff 1989) and it is clear that the private or domestic sphere is by no means less important or inferior in everyday life.[4] Accordingly, in societies with fixed social arrangements (of distribution of power) musical practices might also allow deviation from the established order (Koskoff 1989).

If comparing the traditional musical practices of both research areas (in Kosovo and Slovenia), we see that in the past, the division of repertoire was present either as a result of patriarchal organisation or as a result of ritual residue in everyday life. In the former, the gender division of the repertoire in Kosovo was present at the time it begun to be documented, e.g. before Second World War (see Antoni 1956). After the research work during the 1970s, Munishi came to conclusion that regardless to the evidence of contemporary transformation of rural life, women were traditionally tied to the domestic area and were not in touch with the outside world, which results in a very rich repertoire with little influence from outside the domestic area (Munishi 1979: 6). Typical female repertoire could be classified either by social function or by the circle of life (in vocal music) or by playing instruments that are traditionally attributed to women and are preformed among women. Such is the membranophone instrument *def* (a kind of tambourine with small cymbals on the hoop), which is usually played by women in their private sphere. As per the latter, for example, Zmaga Kumer identifies that some songs from the life circle were reserved for females, such as singing during courting (Kumer 1996: 25–40). Another interesting rite—mourning of the departed—was always performed by a woman (ibid.). Also, the songs of the calendrical cycle (ibid.) sung during various holidays during the year could be divided according to gender (Kumer 1975: 28–40, Klobčar 2008: 463–464). These types of songs are considered part of rites, which may suggest that they are traditionally associated to femininity and are described as so (Klobčar

4 In this research, the division between public and private spheres will be mentioned on several occasions, but the purpose of this research is to explore the relations between the appearance of women in public and their gaining of the economic power.

2008: 463–464.). Also, there are some other types of songs outside of the calendrical cycle (e.g. ballads), which represent historical or ethnic motifs, where—as Marija Klobčar points out—the gender of the interpreter is less determined (Klobčar 2009). The presence of women in instrumental musical practice, on the other hand, is "less expressed" and also less apparent in rural environments (Kovačič 2009). Consequently these practices were not researched as female practices per se, nevertheless the authors point out that women—although they often "underestimated their own musical participation"—did occasionally play instruments (ibid.).

These factors are also common in other countries (see Magrini 2003, Ceribašić 2004) and suggest that in the past the social norms were fixed and the functions in life determined. But, to use Munishi's words, this was possible in the environments with the minimal influence of the outer spatiality. In the lack of this cultural "vacuum" female musical practices seized different opportunities to extend beyond the traditional norms.

WOMEN MUSICIANS AND THE TRANSGRESSION TO PUBLIC SPHERE

As several scholars point out (e.g. in Mediterranean area), musical practices of women that are performed in the public sphere are an important turning point in female practices. It is significant that in some cases, the coming out of the women occurred due to social movements for an importance national cause, such as the political and cultural movement in Corsica in 1970s, researched by Caroline Bithell (Magrini 2003: 45–60) or the emergence of the institutionalisation of Roma musical practices in Macedonia researched by Carol Silverman (Magrini 2003: 133–140).

The political movements in Slovenia (in the second half of the 19th century and beginning of the 20th) and Kosovo (second half of the 20th century) respectively, generated interesting (new) women's practices. Although these occurrences emerged almost a century apart from each other, there are two interesting factors that link these together: the transgression into public sphere and urbanisation of women musicians.

In Slovenian ethnic territory, during the second half of the 19th century, ethnic Slovenians, living under the common Habsburg monarchy, started gathering in the reading rooms of a cultural association called *čitalnice*, where their cultural and political ideas about unifying Slovenians took their roots. The reading rooms were established all over Slovenian ethnic territories and intellectuals, merchants, artisans, in other words urbanites in general gathered there. As a part of the cultural activities in the reading rooms, there were many choirs (mixed, female and male), small ensembles, particularly tamboura ensembles and brass bands. Generally, the reading rooms were filled by those who were eager to learn more about Slovenian culture and literature with enthusiasm and great interest (see Čepič et al. 1979).

The tamboura ensembles initially consisted of men, but soon women joined or (in due course) even established female ensembles. In other words, the ensembles and orchestras offered the possibilities for women to sing and play systematically (Kovačič 2009: 2). Female tamboura ensembles go back to as early as the end of the 19th century (ibid.). In the tamboura ensembles women played instruments in public, a practice that seemed acceptable to the audience; this is in part because historically these orchestras and the associations behind them were significant to people (Tul 1996: 2–3), bearing the representation of the historical endeavour for ethnic and national emancipation and integration. In a way, to use Naila Ceribašić's words, the presentation and the acceptance of women was a part of the imagining of the national family (Ceribašić 2004: 156) and therefore fitted in with the political agenda of that time.

It is interesting that this practice was a "newer" practice, not directly derived from tradition, but rather an urban and also more modern musical practice. This musical practice is connected with urban settings, having in mind that the people that participated in these societies were urbanites (Tul 1996: 2–3). Discussing the appearance of the female instrument players in Croatia at the same period, Naila Ceribašić suggests that tamboura ensembles became a platform where the traditional and modern, regional and class differences are reconciled (Ceribašić 2004: 154). This universality in a way contributed to the persistency and dissemination of this musical practice. After the initial orchestras, this practice continued to flourish well into the 20th century, after the end of the First World War and after the political motivation for *čitalnica* had passed. In the first half of the 20th century, tamboura (male) orchestras were established in rural areas as well (Mučič and Hazler 2012: 20, Dušič Gornik 2008: 14). Very soon, probably influenced by the urban practice, women also joined in (e.g. in area of Artiče, see Dušič Gornik 2008: 14).

The mixed tamboura orchestras continued to be active after the Second World War. There were at least two female ensembles. For example a women's tamboura ensemble in Šmartno ob Paki was established in 1950, by women playing for their own entertainment (Šivic 2003: 171) or the women's tamboura ensemble within the orchestra *Danica* in Ajdovščina, was re-established in 1958 (Tul 1996: 10). Although this paper often emphasises all-female bands, it should be noted that most of tamboura ensembles and orchestras today are usually mixed, but with the majority of female members. Most of these groups do not have any specific denomination that would indicate the mixed structure. There is also a girls' tamboura orchestra in Ormož, which uses the denomination *Dekliški tamburaški orkester Ormož* (Tamboura maid's orchestra Ormož), probably to emphasise the youthfulness of its members.

It is interesting to draw some comparison to Kosovo, where a similar link between political concept, cultural organisation and musical practice took place, though much later. During the 1970s and 1980s many new amateur cultural societies were established in rural areas of Kosovo (as a continuity of similar societies in urban centres that were established after the Second World War). These cultural societies, basically in concordance with state cultural concepts, soon begun to gather the followers of their own political agenda: the political movements for the independence of Kosovo and integration of Albanians within a nation-state. At that time this political concept was very audacious and dangerous and therefore the verbal communication of these ideas was a very delicate matter. Probably this is why the musical practice became significant.

Most of these societies in rural Kosovo had ensembles of *çifteli* (this is a traditional two-string chordophone plucked instrument also originating from a kind of early lute). Contrary to tamboura, the *çifteli* was an instrument that was regarded as unmistakably rural. In rural areas *çifteli* was played solo, by one man, in the male semi-public sphere (in all-men gatherings in the village), usually to accompany a male singer. The most typical repertoire of *çifteli* included heroic or epic songs.

The emergence of the *çifteli* ensembles itself was in a way a modern occurrence. This is evident in several details, such as the augmentation of the ensembles, from one or two instruments (as played traditionally) to larger ensembles of instrument players and singers. Also the musicians were more diverse, age- and gender-wise; usually most of the members were young students or secondary schoolboys and girls. The changes also influenced the repertoire, which became more patriotically oriented (Bejtullahu 2006: 240).

In these ensembles, women were also present, although more as singers and less as instrument players. Nevertheless, their appearance was significant. The engagement of rural women in these ensembles and consequently the transgression of the rural women musicians to the public sphere were possible through two significant social movements: the movement for the stimulation of women's equity (supported by the state) and the strengthening of the movement for national independence. Just like in the above-mentioned case, the transgression was made possible through *çifteli* ensembles or vocal instrumental ensembles of *çifteli*, which also served as places for the transmission of knowledge between generations. Traditionally, *çifteli* associates men's gatherings and singing in men's (public) sphere. At one point in time (around 1970s), due to social movements,[5] it was men that opened their sphere and transmitted their knowledge to women interested to learn this tradition. This is the point when the newer

5 The emergence of *çifteli* ensembles in Kosovo is associated with the new political movements that opted for a change of the political status of Kosovo that appeared at the same time. The repertoire of the *çifteli* ensembles encompassed songs with historical and patriotic topics.

larger formations of *çifteli* were formed. Publicly, it appeared that men and women were equal, but off-stage it was men (as teachers and parents) that controlled the transgression of women into public sphere (Bejtullahu 2006: 235–250).

In other words, *çifteli* ensembles were clearly connected to tradition and people that took part in them regarded themselves as patriots and those responsible for continuing the Albanian national identity in Kosovo. In this concept there was little room for a full-scale modernisation and urbanisation, because people involved in these ensembles believed that these might damage the Albanian national identity and their political movement (Bejtullahu 2006a: 62–75). Because of these reasons, the public appearance of women was regulated: usually they appeared in national costumes, had a modest appearance without make-up, and were static on the stage (Bejtullahu 2006: 248). For some of the female musicians, performing in these ensembles opened the way to popularity and, in due course, to professionalization (which will be presented later).

From the aspect of gender participation, both of the musical practices described—the tamboura orchestras in Slovenia and *çifteli* ensembles in Kosovo—present interesting cases of the transgression of the gender boundaries in the repertoire. While in the case of Slovenia's tamboura orchestras one might argue that women's musical practices took place within the modern processes, in rural areas of Kosovo this transgression took place by the act of appropriation of the male repertoire. Also, it can be argued that the process of transgression by female instrument players takes place as a collective act, often aided by an ideological discourse or a common social movement. In a broader area, in the region, there are also some initial situations, starting points, or—in Naila Ceribašić's words—social footholds that make it possible for women to start playing instruments. Roughly summarised, these footholds are either connected to "nationally-integrated" processed that happen in the broader society, or a result of kinship and family ties, or some stage of awareness of own identity and self even though at the stage of self-negation (Ceribašić 2004: 157–160).

Last of all, it is interesting to see how these musical practices continue to the present day: In the case of tamboura ensembles, it is significant that this female instrumental practice often ceased due to cultural and social conditions and personal reasons, sometimes resurfacing in 1990s due to personal enthusiasm (Šivic 2003: 171, Škvarč in Tul 1996). In the case of Kosovo's *çifteli* ensembles the disappearance (transformation) of the socio-political discourse, together with the vast demographic movements of rural population (migrations) and the introduction of economic factors resulted in the disappearance of a few women instrumental players.

WOMEN'S MUSICAL PRACTICE AND ECONOMICAL POWER

Another important aspect in women's music making is professionalization. For that purpose, the cases from popular music serve as a best example; the most interesting case in Kosovo being the emergence of individual singers that crossed over from traditional to popular music, while in Slovenia the female polka bands are discussed at a greater length. These two cases also show that although the two musical practices might have some common preconditions (e.g. a specific audience, a more or less established musical style and the common challenges of the market economy after the collapse of the socialist system) they can take quite different paths in their development.

Usually professionalization is a continuation of the public performance of women, often together with men.[6] Nevertheless, it does not necessarily mean that the preconditions for performance and music making are the same for both genders. The quest for gaining economical independence and with it the power, has a larger impact in the lives of women, particular-

6 There are also some musical practices that are professional and are limited to women in private or semi-private sphere, such as the mourning of the dead or women tambourine players in weddings, both typical for traditional rituals, in the area of Kosovo and surrounding countries.

ly in the societies where women have a limited access to employment.[7] At first sight, this presents an opportunity for women to gain power in a public space, but, as Heider argues, men still hold the power since they are the real managers of the wealth (Heider 1996: 143). As an illustration of this point, are the family ties between women musicians (singers) and other male musicians. Kinship relations with a male musician seemed like an assurance for a longer and prosperous career for women (Ceribašić 2004: 153).

In the case of Kosovo, the professionalization of village women singers took place in an interesting way, hand in hand with the abandonment of the communist system and introduction of the market economy in 1990–1991. Most of these women come from the *çifteli* ensembles, which means that their background is traditional and with professionalization (unlike women in urban centers of Kosovo) they had to work their way through modernisation as well. In their testimonies, they often mention the role of their fathers and later their husbands, who became their managers and accompanied them to their concerts (Bejtullahu 2006 and 2006a). The presence of a male relative might be interpreted as a consequence of their cultural or even religious upbringing, but after longer research, it was suggested that husbands are involved in this process not only to keep the business in the family but also to keep the family closer (Bejtullahu 2006).

In the case of female Slovenian polka music bands, the presence of the male (and in some cases also a female) relative is also significant. It cannot be ascribed to cultural or religious implications, but rather to the ambition of a parent—usually a father—to support his daughter(s) as a sign of affection (Bejtullahu 2012). As for the playing instruments, there is a disproportion between musicians from Kosovo and Slovenia. For example,[8] vast demographic changes in Kosovo at the turn of the 21th century, as well as

7 One of the most significant cases in the aforementioned literature is the reference to the phases of the process of the professionalization of the Roma singer Esma Redžepova (Magrini 2006: 134–135).

8 The information about instrumental musical practice in Kosovo and Slovenia presented in these chapters was gathered during my research: one part of them is presented in my Master's thesis (Bejtullahu 2006a) while the Slovenian female polka bands is an ongoing research.

the technical simplification of musical reproduction resulted in the attenuation of the instrumental music making, giving the advantage and control of musical performance to those that had the technical means at their disposal. Consequently, female (and also male) *çifteli* players vanished from the musical practice.[9] This happened due to a need for greater mobility of musicians with less costs and, consequently, the lack of a continuous process of transmission of musical practice. As an illustration, many female singers reported that they go to concerts without an ensemble; musical accompaniment is made with the help of technology (pre-recorded CD or a computer programme through a synthesiser). This resulted in an imbalance between female singers (who today represent the majority of female musicians) and female instrument players (who are very rare) (Bejtullahu 2006a).

Women's (as well as men's) instrumental practice is also dependent on continuous transmission of the practice of playing instruments. Female polka bands are derived from the mostly male practice that has developed during the 20th century, and are present in the last two decades. They are represented only by young women that play instruments and sing *narodno-zabavna glasba*, which is the denomination in Slovenian language (pop-folk music, literary: entertaining folk music). The expression Slovenian polka music was suggested by Rajko Muršič (see Bejtullahu 2012).[10] Female polka bands are part of a larger musical practice, typical for the modern yet rural population in Slovenia. These bands emerged around the mid-1990s and today there are at least six bands with all female members. The names of the bands are unmistakably feminine *Vesele Štajerke* (Marrymaking Styria girls), *Navihanke* (Villain girls), *Čebelce* (Little bee girls), *Vražje punce* (Deuced maids), *Iskrice* (Spark girls), *Zapeljivke* (Seductresses), and former *Polka punce* (Polka lassies). The transmission of the female polka musical practice is possible in formal and informal ways. While the latter is possible in private circles (between family members or friends etc.), the former is possible through music schools that have branched out throughout Slovenia in both urban and rural areas. Formal musical education is

9 The instrumental tradition of Kosovo women that is still alive is the playing on *def*, which is still practiced in the weddings in rural areas.

10 Rajko Muršič, personal communication with Alma Bejtullahu, 1 January 2011.

accessible for every young student that has an interest in learning to play an instrument, regardless of gender (Bejtullahu 2012: 266). Through time many girls have learned to play various instruments becoming competent to perform publicly in polka bands. In the last fifteen years, several all-female bands were established (Bejtullahu 2012: 267) and they have continued performing for many years. The transmission of instrument playing from the older generation (of teachers, formal or informal) to the younger generation of women (thus creating bands of young women that play instruments and sing) is one of the means to achieve popularity among the listenership. Consequently, this transmission also contributes to some extent to the continuous musical practice of female polka bands.

Besides that, in professional music making it is important for all the musicians to attract listenership. To serve that purpose, musicians use different levers. Often, as Jennifer Post argues, musicians tend to modify their repertoire in order to maintain a sizeable audience (Post in Koskoff 1989: 106). A good example is the crossover of the former traditional female singers in Kosovo, who at the time of political turmoil in Kosovo became not only famous for presenting traditional Albanian identities but also became emblematic among their listenership (Bejtullahu 2006a). During the course of time, as Kosovo rural areas became more and more modern, the transformation of their music from traditional to a more popular music became a necessity in order to maintain as sizable audience as possible. In the case of polka music the transformations were not as drastic as in Kosovo (Bejtullahu 2012) for the simple reason that polka band music was in its essence already popular music, derived from different music styles.

A "pure" musical performance (meaning the musical sound as it is) is just one part of their performance. For female musicians the music making and the presentation go hand in hand, and this is a norm that is established with female musicians and also with their audience.[11] This kind of gender-specific norm is not new in music, having in mind that marking masculine and feminine traits through music was common also in the past, e.g. in the singing abilities presented on-stage (Ahlquist 2004: 10).

11 Sonja Hercog, personal communication with Alma Bejtullahu, 30 September 2011.

It is interesting that female musicians have recognized and try to address a constant request of the audience for the presentation of novelties. They had a lot to do with their feminine visual representation. Kosovar rural singers, that were represented as individual and established singers, went (and still go) through vast visual transformations which is a complete opposite of the traditional aesthetic they have represented in 1980s. Most of the singers of the (once) patriotic and traditional music style, now in their forties and fifties, have very modern styling, they undergo make-overs and in general try to adopt a more youthful look, which is a complete opposite of the traditional aesthetic they have represented in 1980s. It is interesting that male musicians did not drastically transform their appearance. Similar transformations take place in the Slovenian polka music scene. Slovenian polka girls are more aware of their appearance than their male counterparts: they started using colourful costumes and more recently they introduce themed-presentations during concerts, which include choreographed dances with accompanying costumes and scenarios. Usually one of the members has a task to act as a host and an animator of the concert.[12]

There is an unavoidable first impression of female bands which is a display of their femininity or even sexuality. The issue of women that assume their musical roles by heightening their sexuality has often been addressed by various scholars, such as Elen Koskoff. She argues that in the West women's musical talent is often "defined in terms of cultural expectations of female sexuality" (Koskoff 1989: 6). Using Elizabeth Wood's findings that women must serve a linked economic and erotic interests of a dominant (meaning male-centered) culture, Koskoff argues that in societies where males are the main patrons of musical performances or where male-dominated economic spheres call for young female performers, musical behaviour that heightens their sexuality is a norm (ibid.).

However, inter-gender relations are not very strict; Koskoff proposes various categories in inter-gender relations in music performance allowing the possibility, that women who find their way perform within this norm but at the same time undermine or even challenge it (Koskoff 1989: 10). Often

12 Ibid.

they take up these norms in order to achieve other ends, such as popularity and fame. This proposition in a way coincides with the female musicians' point of view according to which the existing norms are acceptable but at the same time they feel that they have control over their performance. They consider that their gender representation and display of sexuality is specifically theirs and their trump card, because in their circle it is considered that their practice is a "market niche" and—compared to their male counterpart—gives them an advantage.

CONCLUSION

In the terms of musical practice, there are several points that are taken into an account: in case of *çifteli* musical practice, which opened the way for Kosovo women from rural areas, it was not sufficient to establish a continuous instrumental practice. On one hand, the emancipation of women, as well as the professionalization of women musicians under the conditions of the free market could be a "fertilising agent" for an instrumental career; on the other hand this also forced the laws of commerce to take over as the migration and mobility of people required the women to perform with fewer expenses. Consequently the instrumental bands are slowly disappearing, while women did not negotiate a role in taking hold of power, which only suggests that—in Koskoff's terms—the performers maintain the established social and sexual order.

The significance of the economical factor is evident also in women's instrumental musical practices in Slovenia. The tamboura ensembles once were a platform for negotiation regarding the new norms, today, as a not particularly lucrative activity; they are the platform for individual confirmation. At the same time, polka female musicians that perform in conformity with economical parameters achieved the shift of power in musical production and performance. By the means of transmission of instrumental interpretation, women have the upper hand and are in control of what they perform and how they perform (which is in conformity with sexually established norms). In the terms of the broader context, the story of women musicians in Kosovo and Slovenia is also a story of how a society modernises. Both the societies researched have experienced modernisation as a process that is absorbed from the outside, noticeably through urban settings. This is particularly important when women seek to reach out for a broader listenership. As seen in the case of *çifteli* ensembles in Kosovo, the strictly traditional orientation of the repertoire caused women to reach out mostly to the rural public sphere and only later, with the loosening of this norm, they were able to keep up with their listenership. On the other hand the tamboura ensembles that emerged as a new and more universal practice, have achieved an interesting and almost eternal status among Slovenian musicians. Finally, as both cases indicate, the modernisation of music can proceed up to a point, while the modernisation of the appearance and with that the rousing of the visual attractiveness is a constant process.

REFERENCES

Ahlquist, Karen

2004 Masculinity and Legitimacy on the English Musical Stage: The Mature Male, 1800–1845. *Women and Music: A Journal of Gender and Culture* 8: 1–21.

Antoni, Lorenc

1956 *Folklori muzikor shqiptar*. Prishtinë: Shtëpia botuese "Milladin Popoviq."

Bejtullahu, Alma

2006 Female singers in rural Kosovo – from the domestic to the public domain. In: Saurer, Edith et al. (eds.), *Women's movements: networks and debates in post-communist countries in the 19th and 20th centuries*. Köln, Weimar, Wien: Böhlau Verlag, 235–250.

2006a *Glasba na Kosovu ob osamosvojitvenih prizadevanjih* (master's thesis). Ljubljana: University of Ljubljana, Faculty of Arts, Department of Musicology.

2012 La polka slovène, entra tradition et modernité. *Ethnologie française* 42, 2012: 263–272.

Ceribašić, Naila

2004 Između etnomuzikoloških i društvenih kanona: povijesni izvori o sviračicama narodnih glazbala u Hrvatskoj. In: Ambrešić Kirin, Renata, and Tea Škokić (eds.), *Između roda i naroda. Etnološke i folklorističke studije*. Zagreb: Centar za ženske studije, 147–163.

Čepič, Zdenko, et al.

1979 *Zgodovina Slovencev*. Ljubljana: Cankarjeva založba.

Dušič Gornik, Breda

2008 Prva glasbila so izdelali kar sami. *Živa. Priloga dolenjskega lista* 7 (1) januar 2008: 14.

Eriksen, Thomas Hylland

2009 *Mali kraji, velike teme*. Maribor: Aristej.

Heider, Karl G.,
1996 *Seeing anthropology: Cultural anthropology through film.* Boston: Allyn and Bacon.

Klobčar, Marija
2008 Kresne pesmi kot razumevanje obrednega. In: Slavec Gradišnik, Ingrid (ed.), *Čar izročila. Zapuščina Nika Kureta* (1906–1995). Ljubljana: Založba ZRC, 457–484.
2009 Hidden behind the transcriptions (manuscript, submitted for publication).

Koskoff, Ellen (ed.)
1989 *Women and Music in Cross-Cultural Perspective.* Urbana and Chicago: University of Illinois Press.

Kovačič, Mojca
2009 Gender relations in instrumental folk music in Slovenia (manuscript, submitted for publication).

Kumer, Zmaga
1975 *Pesem slovenske dežele.* Maribor: Obzorja.
1996 *Vloga, zgradba, slog slovenske ljudske pesmi.* Ljubljana: Znanstvenoraziskovalni center SAZU.

Magrini, Tulia
2003 *Music and Gender: Perspectives from the Mediterranean.* Chicago and London: The University of Chicago Press.

Mučič, Tina, and Vito Hazler (eds.)
2012 *Naše kulturno bogastvo.Vrednotenje nesnovne kulturne dediščine.* Litija: Center za razvoj.

Munishi, Rexhep
1979 *Këndimi i femrave të Podgurit.* Prishtinë: Instituti Albanologjik i Prishtinës.

Sugarman, Jane
1997 *Engendering song. Singing and subjectivity at Prespa Albanian weddings.* Chicago and London: The University of Chicago Press.

Šivic, Urša
2003 Ljudska pesem, glasba in ples v Šmarski okolici. In: Šalej, Matjaž, and Emil Šterbenk (eds.), *Šmartno ob Paki. Zbornik raziskovalnega tabora ERICa v letih 2001 in 2002*. Velenje: Erico, 161–189.

Tul, Vlasta
1996 *Tamburice v Šturjah in Ajdovščini zvenijo že stoletje.* Katalog k razstavi. Ajdovščina, Nova Gorica: Glasbena šola Vinko Vodopivec, Pokrajinski arhiv.

Selena Rakočević

PAST IN THE PRESENT: CONTEMPORARY MANIFESTATIONS OF THE CUSTOM *REVENA*

ABSTRACT

The *revena* custom was widespread among the Serbian population all over Vojvodina (northern part of Serbia) until the middle of the 20th century. It has been practiced by women exclusively as one segment of the carnival celebrations. During the *revena* all limits of the women's behavior imposed by the patriarchal society could be exceeded. The content of this paper is based on the *revena* custom which was video recorded in the village of Taraš in April 2008. The focus of the paper will be directed toward the examination of the forms and semantics of the women's behavior during the *revena* in the past, but also in the contemporary village society of this part of Serbia.

Key words: *revena*, women custom, theatrical presentations, Vojvodina

INTRODUCTION

The concept of folklore could be interpreted in various ways with bundles of connotations and issues. The aim of this ethnographical paper is to demonstrate one of the notions of folklore as tradition, i.e. as a relative and relational process of holding on to previous times in which cultural forms are being creatively renewed and reinterpreted. Even the context could be changed within the contemporary society, connotations and functions of particular traditional forms could keep their basic meanings from the past. One of them is the *revena* custom from Vojvodina. The term *revena* (literally "co-partnership") is of Persian-Turkish origin and generally refers to the union and partnership of a particular group of people, but also the joint covering of all community costs (Milosavljević 1971: 335). As a custom, *revena* was transferred to the Balkans by the Turks and was found in the wider area of Serbia, Bosnia and Herzegovina and parts of Croatia (the region of Lika) until the middle of the 20th century (Milosavljević 1971: 335). In Croatia, Bosnia and Herzegovina and the southern areas of Serbia, it was mostly practiced by males (Malešević 1996: 73). However, according to ethnographical sources, in the northern areas of Serbia i.e. Vojvodina, *revena* was exclusively a female custom and has been spread among the Serbian population all over the region,[1] but also across its borders in Serbian villages in the Northern part of Romania (Asanović 2008: 40–47; Bosić 1996: 214–218; Malešević 1996: 142–145; Milosavljević 1971: 335–337).

The female custom *revena* was practiced on the so-called Clean Monday (the first Monday of the period of Lent) as one segment of the carnival celebrations. Although it was associated with the dates of the Christian calendar, there is no data that the Orthodox Church authorities in Vojvodina suppressed any of the festivities which were practiced at the beginning of Lent, including *revena*. It could be said that they have been simply ignored by the village priests.

Even nowadays, carnival celebrations in the eastern part of Vojvodina—Banat can last for several days. They can be organized in various forms one of which is the *revena*. After a so-called big clean of the kitchen, which included fat dishes especially, women would gather together in the house of one of them and start their feast (each women brought a lot of food and alcoholic drinks). At one feast—*revena*, there were ten to twenty women from the same part of the village (mostly neighbours and relatives), which means that those people knew each other very well so they could behave freely during the celebration. The only man who was allowed to join was the player (bagpiper or accordion player). Men generally avoided coming to a *revena*, because they would be exposed to highly unpleasant and even rude jokes by the women participants (Milosavljević 1971: 337). The musicians, however, had a special status during the feast. They were paid for their playing and they could consume unlimited food and drink. On the

1 The Autonomous Province of Vojvodina is the multiethnic and multicultural province of Serbia. This administrative region is divided by the Danube and Tisza rivers into: Bačka in the northwest, Srem in the southwest and Banat in the east.

Fig. 1: Participants of the revena *custom. The town of Kikinda, 1968. Photo: National museum, Kikinda.*

other hand, they were not allowed to talk in public about what was happening during the celebration.

During the *revena* all limits of the women's behaviour imposed by patriarchal society could be exceeded. Beside the collective, unlimited overeating and even getting drunk, the obligatory part of this custom was theatrical performances by masked women. Different from other carnival masks, which could be various (Marjanović 1999: 246), all masks in *revena* were anthropoid. The standard characters performed by the masked women were: a pregnant bride, a young childish bridegroom, an orthodox priest and a dead man. Beside masked characters, the important guests in each *revena* were also two godmothers (the old one, godmother from last year's manifestation and the new one).

The themes of those performances could be various, but constant theatrical motives appeared: giving the presents to the godmothers of the *revena*, introduction of the new members of a "clan," diverse wedding scenes as well as the so-called lamenting of the dead. No matter what the content, all the theatrical presentations included lascivious behaviour, off-colour stories and gestures with metaphorical sexual connotations.

While it is almost forgotten in the regions of Srem and Bačka, the *revena* custom is still practiced in the villages of Taraš and Kumane in the Northern Banat. The aim of this paper is to present the *revena* custom which has been video recorded in the village of Taraš in April 2008. The focus will be directed toward the examination of the forms and semantics of the lascivious theatrical presentations of the women during the *revena* in the contemporary village society of this part of Serbia. The questions that will be considered are: to what extent the *revena* custom retains its forms, connotations and functions from the past? What does it mean to the local community of women? Does it function as a kind of an archaism or does it assume new forms and meanings? On the other hand, as one kind of the contemporary folklore manifestations, what are the possible ways of its continuation in the future?

THE PAST IN THE PRESENT: THE CONTEMPORARY MANIFESTATIONS OF THE *REVENA* CUSTOM IN THE VILLAGE OF TARAŠ

The village of Taraš is populated by a small Serbian community (the population is approximately 1000 people). The place is only several kilometres away from the nearby town of Zrenjanin, but the connecting road is very narrow and bad because it was built on the embankment (all around is a swampy terrain). Daily bus connections exist but include only morning and evening services.

The inhabitants are mostly farm workers who cultivate their own fields, but some of them also work in Zrenjanin. The gender division of the working processes are still very intensive, which mean that the hard jobs in the fields are done by men while women are busy with housekeeping and gardening. Once a week most of the families sell their products at Zrenjanin's markets. Beside the fact that the traditional age limits are exceeded, the marriage customs even nowadays dictate that the bridegrooms should be in their early twenties. In most of the cases the new couple stay in the family

Fig. 2: The village of Taraš. Map: Ivan Potić, 2009. Source: Wikipedia.org/Military geographical institute, 1988.

house so several generations live in one place. The hierarchical order between generations means that all the hard jobs are taken by younger people. On the other hand, relationships between sexes dictated that women were always put at the weaker point. The position of women in such big families was certainly hard and restricted. Divorces are still very rare and several women explained that this is primarily because of economical reasons.

The *revena* custom held in the village of Taraš in April 2008 has kept all the segments which were recorded in the ethnographical literature. However, it is hard to trace this custom diachronically through periods of the last century because all of the ethnographic data were presented as a kind of, I will use the term of Max Weber, "ideal-typical" presentation (according to Đurić 1997: 15). However, compared with the written descriptions, it could be mentioned that no "new" elements have been recorded and that *revena* held in 2008 has kept all of its previous features. The female participants of the *revena* were mostly housewives, but they also included one lady-teacher and several saleswomen. Even all of the women were very involved in the celebration, several of them distinguished themselves from the group by their organizational and leading skills as well as a talent for theatrical expression.

The celebration begun in the early afternoon and lasted until the late night. Two female ethnomusicology students from Belgrade, as well as myself joined the group from the beginning. Our visit to the village and intention to record the feast had been announced several days earlier by a phone call to one of the women. Even though the three of us were in the village of Taraš for the first time and, on the other hand, *revena* participants did not have any other foreign guests during celebrations in previous years, the women accepted us spontaneously. We tried to be invisible and to observe and record all the activities from "the corners," intending to have as little effect as possible on the spontaneous behaviour of the women and not to jeopardize the course of the celebration. Although the *revena* participants were aware of their unusual behaviour that would be strongly condemned in everyday contexts, they retained the freedom and spontaneity in all their actions during the feast despite the observers. The fact that all of us were

Fig. 3: Departure of the godmothers. The village of Taraš, 2008. Photo: Selena Rakočević.

female possibly facilitated our field research. The whole event started with the collective departure of the godmothers. As in all the other actions, the departure of the godmothers was organized in an amusing way which this year meant that the godmothers should sit in the baby chairs. The baby chairs were fixed to the back side of the motor cultivator which was driven by one of the women.

In the house of one of the women, who for many years had given the abandoned, but well-preserved family house for the *revena* celebration, two players were already waiting for the cheerful procession: an accordion player, who had participated for more than ten years in *revena* and a bass player, who was participating for the first time.

The feast in the house began with the singing of *bećarci*, which lasted for approximately half an hour. *Bećarac* (plural: *bećarci*) is a traditional vocal-instrumental genre, whose form implies double-versed lyrics with improvised textual content (Matović 1998: 44). Literally the term *bećarac* refers to "the song of the young dandy fellow," although it could be performed by both genders. Through using several, but mostly a one tune-model (Matović 1998: 45–47) and verses following one another, one performance of the *bećarci* songs could tell a whole series of different stories, the content of which often depends on the momentary inspiration of the singer. Newly-composed music hits mostly from the period of the 1960s, 1970s and 1980s followed the performance of the *bećarci*. Women ordered their favourite songs from the musicians freely, so hits followed one after another spontaneously. Women were actively singing with the musicians all the time, mostly knowing all the lyrics, rocking to the beat, patting, and often climbing onto the seat cushions placed along the tables. This time I will not analyze the musical interpretation. For most of the songs, however, it could be said that they represent the "evergreen" of the newly composed music. Among them are: "Zlatibore pitaj Taru" (Zlatibor, ask Tara), "Odakle si, sele?" (Where are you from, sister?), "Mostovi na Morači" (Bridges over the river Morača), "Sedamdeset i dva dana" (Seventy-two days), "Lepa vodeničarka" (Pretty woman from the mill), "Davorike daj-

Fig. 4: Female singers and musicians at the revena. *The village of Taraš, 2008. Photo: Selena Rakočević.*

ke" (Davorike dajke), "Zorice, Zorule" (Zorica, Zorule), "Uzmi sve što ti život pruža" (Take all what life gives you) and others.

The segment of the custom which is called "giving presents to the godmothers" was the next one. The gifts were small purses, red lipsticks, sexy underwear and cheap jewellery. During this action the players performed another popular vocal-instrumental genre called *cajke*. *Cajka* (plural: *cajke*) is a vocal-instrumental genre, whose form is similar to the form of the *bećarac* but the textual content is exclusively lascivious (Zrilić 2004: 11–14, Forry 2011: 214–215). The term for the genre is an obscene nickname for females. The *cajke* songs could be performed only within the small circle of people during the late hours of various private or family celebrations. Very rarely they are performed in the village pubs (*kafanas*), mostly among men (Forry 2011: 215). At the *revena* celebration, they have been performed only during the giving of presents to the godmothers, by using several popular and well known verses. They were sung by both the musicians and some of the women. This segment of the custom lasted less than ten minutes. Immediately after they received gifts, the godmothers were served the main dish in the ceremonial way. It was mixed meat shaped into the form of a penis. This segment of the custom was not followed by music, but only lascivious jokes.

After the dinner was served, several theatrical presentations were organized. Considering the fact that the same female characters participated in them, the theatrical presentations followed one after another. They consisted of humorous dialogues and acting, but without any music.

The introduction of the new members took place through the action of their "baptism." The "priest" imitated the orthodox ritual but in a humorous way and again with direct sexual connotations. The holy image was replaced by the erotic photo of a man, which had to be kissed, the ritual bath with marking the sexual organ with the cleaning brush, and finally there was cutting the hair. After they have baptised the new lady-member,

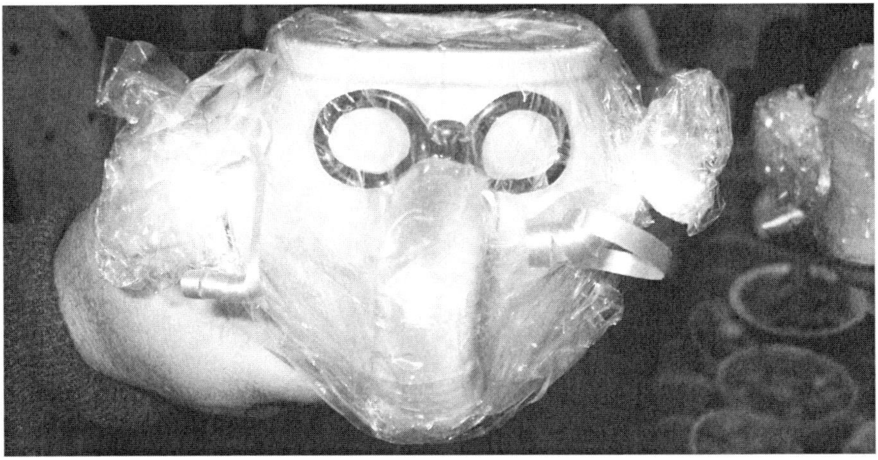

Fig. 5: Gift for a godmother: a funny cap. The village of Taraš, 2008. Photo: Selena Rakočević.

the "priest" realized that the bass player was also at the *revena* for the first time. So he tried to baptize him. This segment of the custom was accompanied by rampant, lascivious jokes and laughter by all of the participants. At first, the bass player complained with a laugh and refused to be baptized, but in the end, however, he relented. It must be noted that despite the level of immediate and banal sexual metaphor, the whole act did not seem for us, field researchers as the observers of the ritual, vulgar and unpleasant. This impression is, I believe, influenced by the cheerful mood of the participants and their directness and proximity in their contact with us.

After the act of the baptism, the theatrical segment of the celebration continued with the "wedding." Next to the "priest," there were the "groom," "pregnant bride" and witnesses. After a humorous examination of when exactly, how and with whom the "pregnant bride" conceived a baby, which took place through humorous dialogue full of ambiguous connotations be-

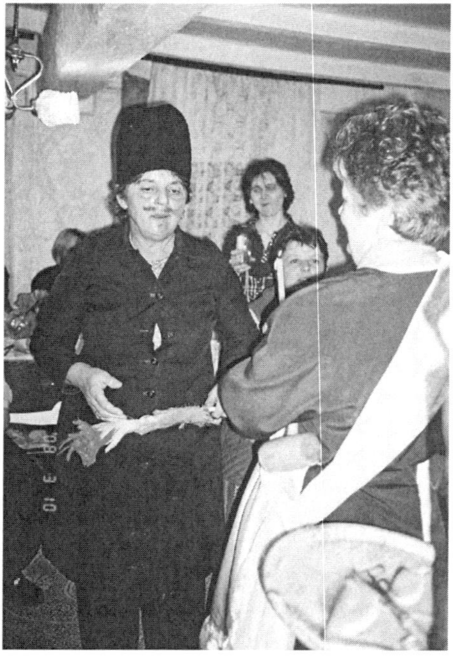

Fig. 6: Baptizing. The village of Taraš, 2008. Photo: Selena Rakočević.

tween the "priest" and the others, this segment of the celebration ended with a ceremonial kiss between the bride and the groom.

The theatrical segment of the *revena* custom finished shortly before midnight. After that, the celebration continued until the early morning hours with singing newly composed music hits. Some of the songs were performed several times during the night. The women did not dance because the space in the room was confined.

CONCLUSION

The steady structural form of the *revena* could be easily explained by the physical isolation of the village of Taraš. The possible connotations of the *revena* as a kind of an archaic ritual with the general ideas of the potential benefits of imitating ritual actions, which were notated as dominant semantic dimensions of the *revena* during the first half of the 20th century (Bosić 1996: 216–217), have been all, not forgotten, but pushed into the deep background of the performers' minds. That's why the statements as "It should be done" or "It is good to be performed" are still the part of the local semantic discourse of this custom.

However, the connotations of pure entertainment and personal female self-expression are the main semantic categories of its contemporary manifestations. In spite of the fact that the common characteristics of the other contemporary theatrical customs in the central Balkans and Serbia, for example processions of *koledari* (Christmas carollers) or *lazarice* (Lazar's Saturday female procession), could be summed up in the tendencies for realistic dramatic presentations, reduction of the metaphorical meanings and general simplification (Antonijević 1997: 177), in the *revena* which was held in the village of Taraš in 2008, the exaggerating in all of the segments of the custom has been saved as its basic aesthetical principle. That's why the theatrical manifestations of this custom should be understood as a kind of inverted reproduction of the repressive everyday reality of the women not only at the level of the rural social community, but also within the complex family and matrimony relations in this area, which still keep the forms of the previous times (Malešević 1996: 76). Within the female community of the village of Taraš, the *revena* custom still functions not as an archaism, a museum artefact, but rather as an important emotional release from the oppressive hierarchical conditions and as a potential corrective to outdated social relations at the local level.

Considering the question "What to do with folklore?" one can say that in the case of the contemporary manifestations of the *revena* custom, a possible answer is to encourage its continuation in its changing aspects. As a unique form of the local cultural practice in which the theatrical performances have a prominent place, the *revena* custom has certain potentials as a possible touristic commodity, but only on condition that the village community are interested in that. Besides consulting them, the first step in the consideration of this possibility would be introducing *revena* to the wider public. On the other hand, the theatrical presentations are just one segment of the complex structure and semantics of the *revena* custom. Within the patriarchal social organization of the family with the repressive position of the female members, which is still dominant in the village community, the *revena* custom functions as a kind of emotional release and a way of balancing the asymmetrical gender relations. Through extremely lascivious jokes, masks and theatrical presentations which keep the exact forms from the past, female participants of the *revena* custom temporarily cross the forbidden line that separates acceptable from unacceptable social behaviour. Along with the standard form of the custom, the grotesque roles of the participants which reverse their everyday social positions could be interpreted as the key element of the basic semantics of this custom. For the female participants of the *revena*, it could be said with certainty that they do not feel as if they are trapped in folklore, but, quite the opposite, that one of its contemporary manifestations allows them to feel and behave freely without oppressive social restrictions. The *revena* custom gives to the village women a sense of freedom, an opportunity to overcome the frustrations of their everyday reality and, last but not least, a chance to express their own sexuality without specified limits. If we turn back to the question "What to do with folklore?" considering not only the *revena* but also all other contemporary folklore manifestations, the possible general answers should be traced in the first place by the communities themselves, which should have a decisive role in defining the paths of the continuation or promotion of their own heritage (Ceribašić 2009: 131–132).

REFERENCES

Antonijević, Dragoslav
1997 *Dromena*. Posebna izdanja. Beograd: Srpska akademija nauka i umetnosti, Balkanološki institut.

Asanović, Srđan
2008 Revena u Kikindi. *Etnoumlje* 3: 40–47.

Bosić, Mila
1996 *Godišnji običaji Srba u Vojvodini*. Novi Sad: Muzej Vojvodine & Prometej.

Ceribašić, Naila
2009 Novi val promicanja nacionalne baštine: UNESKO-va 'Konvencija o očuvanju nematerijalne kulturne baštine' i njezina implementacija. In: Talam, Jasmina (ed.), *Šesti međunarodni simpozij 'Muzika u društvu'. Zbornik radova*. Sarajevo: Muzikološko društvo FbiH & Muzička akademija u Sarajevu, 122–135.

Đurić, Mihajlo
1997 *Problemi sociološkog metoda*. Beograd: Službeni list & Tersit.

Forry, Mark
2011 *Saglasje tradicije i kulture u tamburaškoj muzici Vojvodine*. Novi Sad: Prometej.

Malešević, Miroslava
1996 Revena – ženski praznik. *Etno-kulturološki zbornik* 2: 142–145.

Marjanović, Vesna
1999 Fenomen maske u narodnoj kulturi stanoviništva Banata. *Etno-kulturološki zbornik* 5: 243–256.

Matović, Ana
1998 *Bećarac u Vojvodini. Oblici i razvoj*. Novi Sad: Matica srpska.

Milosavljević, Milivoj
1971 Revena. Običajno-pravno udruživanje ljudi u jelu i piću. *Rad vojvodjanskih muzeja* 20: 335–338.

Zrilić, Zlatko (ed.)
2004 *Opet cajka iz Novoga Sada*. Sremska Mitrovica: Sirmijumart.

Zlata Marjanović

BETWEEN FOLKLORE AND FOLKLORISM: (HI)STORY OF ONE TUNE IN MUSIC TRADITION OF SLOVENIA, CROATIA, SERBIA AND MONTENEGRO

ABSTRACT

This paper is focused on one tune which from the 19th century becomes a part of the music traditions of Croatia, Slovenia, Serbia and Montenegro. Beginning with the Franjo Ksaver Kuhač's description of the initial creation of the tune (from 1833), it is possible to reveal one of the ways in which a new form of folklore is made: the folklorism. Using the existing musical transcriptions and sound recordings, one can learn how the very same folklorism becomes a part of folklore.

Key words: "Još Hrvatska ni propala", spread and role of one tune, folklore, folklorism

INTRODUCTION

This paper attempts to reconstruct the (hi)story of one Tune in a wide geographical area and in a long timespan (during a 179-year period).[1] With its interesting historical, social and musical journey, this Tune is manifested in the musical tradition of Slovenia, Croatia, Serbia and Montenegro:[2]

1. "Još Hrvatska ni propala" (Croatia still isn't ruined), Zagreb, Croatia; Kuhač 1881: 361, 362,
2. "Kiša pada, trava raste, to je godina" (Rain falls, Grass is growing, it is the Year), Croatia; Kuhač 1881: 361,

1 For better understanding of this text, this tune will be written in this paper with first letter capitalised.

2 There are probably more areas in which the Tune had been sung, but it seems that the collected examples are sufficient for the needs of this paper.

3. "Svirka" (Playing), Krapina, Pregrada, Croatia; Hrvatska tradicijska kultura 2004: No. 29,
4. "Kiša pada, trava raste, gora zelena" (Rain falls, Grass is growing, green Mountain), Gospić, Lika, Croatia; Stepanov 1956: No. 81,
5. "Ljubio se bjeli golub sa golubicom" (A white Pigeon was kissing a Hen-pigeon), Peroj, Istria, Croatia; Vasiljević 1965: No. 542,
6. "Trojka" (Dance in three), Hotiza, Prekmurje, Slovenia; Ramovš 1996: No. 6,
7. "Trojka" (Dance in three), Prekmurje, Slovenia; *Zvočnost slovenskih pokrajin* 1991: No. 6 and *Ansambel Trutamora Slovenica* ... 2011,
8. "Našla sem ga, našla sem ga, zlato jabolko" (I found, I found, a gold Apple), Semič, White Carniola, Slovenia; Tomc 1948: 58,
9. "Krivka" (Crooked Dance), Banat, Vojvodina, Serbia; Kuhač 1880: No. 1176,
10. "Poranila devojčica golube da hrani" (The Girl got up early to feed the Pigeons), Vojvodina, Serbia; Radio televizija Srbije, Produkcija gramofonskih ploča, Organizacija muzičkih autora Srbije SOKOJ 2003: No. 13,
11. "Neko voli seljančicu, neko gospođicu" (Someone likes Peasant-girl, Someone likes little Miss), Ćićevac, Rasina district, Serbia; Vasiljević s.a.,
12. "Pajun pase, trava raste, pauniću moj" (Peacock's eating, Grass is growing, oh, my Peacock), Gornja Lastva, Boka Kotorska Bay, Montenegro; Vasiljević 1965: No. 211,
13. "Paun leti da poleti, paunići moj" (Peacock's fly to take fly, oh, my Peacock), Kotor, Boka Kotorska Bay, Montenegro; *Klapa Karampana* ... 2009,
14. "Uz trpezu, niz trpezu, sivi sokole" (Up and down the Table, grey Falcon), Dobrota, Boka Kotorska Bay, Montenegro; Vasiljević 1965: No. 238,
15. "Ja uranih i podranih rano na vodu" (I got up early and went early for the Water), Bijela, Boka Kotorska Bay, Montenegro; Vasiljević 1965: No. 202,
16. "Slavjo poje u lugove, bješe tamna noć" (Nightingale sang in the Wood, it was a dark Night), Prčanj, Boka Kotorska Bay, Montenegro; Vasiljević 1965: No. 293,

17. "Vrgom okom u dumbravi, zamjerih krune" (I looked in grove, I saw the Crown), Prčanj, Boka Kotorska Bay, Montenegro; Vasiljević 1965: No. 293a,
18. "Polećela dva andjela oba sa neba" (Two Angels flew through, both from the Sky), Bijela, Boka Kotorska Bay, Montenegro; Marjanović Krstić 1998: No. 86,
19. "Počela dva andjela oba sa neba" (Two Angels flew through, both from the Sky), Budva, Montenegro; Marjanović 2002a: 134.

There are probably more musical transcriptions and sound recordings. This list of tunes demonstrates that the Tune arrived as folklorism but it became a part of folklore. The aim of this paper is to examine how and why the Tune appears and becomes a part of folklore and what is important for all those people who find this long-lived Tune as an equal part of their tradition.

TUNE'S "FIRST LIFE"

During research for the origin of this Tune, we are coming to two crucial "points:" to the beginning of the 19th century and to the cultural and historical past of Croatia. Briefly, that was a period of national revival, also known as the Illyrian Movement. Followers of this movement were representing the unity of all South Slavs and they demonstrated their ideas in literary, cultural, social and political fields.[3] In addition, in 1835 the first Illyrian *budnica* (reveille) "Još Hrvatska ni propala" was publicly performed (Kuhač 1881: 363).[4] The author of the lyrics was Ljudevit Gaj (1809–1872), and of the Tune—this very one, which is in common with

3 Followers of the Illyrian Movement idea reckon that South Slav people are ancestors of the old Balkan Illyrians and they attempted to join all South Slav people under the Illyrian name (to create a unique literature based on a mutual standard language and orthography etc.). This has been explained in the best way through literary forms and consequently appeals occurred with national content, epic forms, etc. The Illyrian revival was forbidden in 1843 by the authorities, but despite that ban, poets continued creating in that manner until the 1860s (see more in Cvijić 1991: 505, Dvorniković 2000: 870, Andreis 1966: 338–339 and Cvetko 1960).

4 *Budnica* (reveille) is a popular song, and in conformity with its title, is intended for awaking patriotic, political conscience of the masses.

1553. Još Hrvatska ni propala.

Andante agitato ♩ = 84. Iz Zagreba. (*Od god. 1833.*)

Još Hrvatska ni propala,
Dok mi živimo.
Visoko se bude stala,
Kad ju zbudimo.
Ak' je dugo tvrdo spala,
Jača hoće bit.
Ak' je sada u snu mala,
Hoće s' prostranit.

Većput sanja čudne senje
Sladke radosti,
Kada joj se kažu tenje
Jake mladosti,
Drugda pako magle crne,
Nju obstiraju,
Kada sestre njoj nevjerne
Nju zapiraju.

Jednoč vidi županije
Sve ponovljene,
Stare slavne sve banije
Snova stvorene.
Vidi, čuje Gorotance
Kranjce dolazit,
I s Hrvati neprestance
Tako govorit:

Oj Hrvati, braćo mila,
Čujte našu rieč,
Razdružit nas neće sila,
Baš nikakva već.
Nas je njegda jedna majka
Draga rodila,
S jednim nas je, Bog joj plati,
Mliekom dojila.

Kako ćemo majki bolje
Sad zahvaliti,
Neg da budmo jedne volje,
Svi sjediniti.
Jal i nazlob njoj su sine
Sve razdružili,
Stare slave domovine
Diku srušili.

Nij' li skoro skrajne vrieme,
Da ju zvisimo,
Ter da tudje težko breme,
Iz nas bac'mo.
Stari smo i mi Hrvati,
Nismo zabili,
Da su naši pravi brati,
Zlo probavili.

Jednoč čuje svoje sine,
Glasno pjevati,
Složno glase u visine,
Tako dizati:
Braćo! danas kolo vodi,
Danak svetkuje,
Hrvatska se preporodi,
Sin se raduje.

U kolu su svi Hrvati
Stare državе,
Stare slave vjerni svati,
Z Like, Krbave.
Kranjci, Štajer, Gorotanci,
I Slavonija,
Bosna, Srbi, Istrijanci,
Ter Dalmacija.

Svi Hrvati se rukuju,
I spoznavaju.
Istinski se sad kušuju,
Rieč si davaju.
Neka znadu svieta puci,
Njihov novi svez,
Hvalit će ju vnukov vnuci
Njihov narod ves.

Nuder braćo! čaše s vinom,
Sad napunite.
Zdravicu hrvatskim sinom,
Vjernim napijte.

Neka živi naša sloga,
Svaki pravi Slav,
Pravi sinko roda svoga
Neka bude zdrav.

(Spjevao Dr. Ljudevit Gaj.)

Fig. 1: Reveille, Zagreb, Croatia; Kuhač 1881: 361, 362.

all the listed musical transcriptions and sound recordings—composer Ferdo Livadić (1799–1879).[5]

The text writer mentioned, Ljudevit Gaj, described to the Croatian ethnomusicologist Franjo Ksaver Kuhač how the Tune emerged. To benefit romanticism (the language and cultural revival and movements close to the patriotic enthusiasm) the first words of this *budnica* occurred to Gaj in 1833, while he was riding on his sleigh to Samobor, to visit his friend Ferdo Livadić in order to awaken the Croats "from their dreaming" (Kuhač 1881: 362). He wished to write a poem that would start with the exact words "Još Hrvatska nij' propala."

During the ride, his thoughts were interrupted by a sound of some faraway folk music, where he only could recognize the "droning of a double bass" (Kuhač 1881: 362). Rhythm of that droning matched with the meter of Gaj's verse, so while in the sleigh, he already figured out the first strophe. In order not to forget his brain child, Gaj literary "burst in" to Livadić's home, writing the song and droning aloud the tune "or better to say, rhythm of a double bass" (Kuhač 1881: 362). He also transferred his enthusiasm to Livadić, who immediately sat at the piano and tried to reproduce Gaj's tune. That is how the *budnica* "Još Hrvatska ni propala" originated. In order to confirm the authenticity of Gaj's story, it was not hard for Kuhač to look for, find and, in the end transcribed in Samobor, in 1869 "one Croatian dance," which in its bass part, also contained recognizable motives of the alleged, first Illyrian *budnica*.[6]

Sounds "of some faraway music" that Gaj mentioned (Kuhač 1881: 362), however, prove that the Tune already existed in the folk practices of a wider area, and that Livadić only adapted it for Gaj's lyrics. So, the origin of the first Illyrian *budnica* (and the Tune), according to research of ethnologist

5 This artist creates under the influence of Ljudevit Gaj's ideas and his opus is a specific answer to the Western European events and national revivals that were ongoing at that time all over the Europe.

6 See more in Kuhač 1881: 362–363.

and archaeologist Stjepan Sremac (Sremac 2010)[7] and ethnomusicologist Svanibor Pettan, is possible to find even in Poland.[8]

Regardless of origins of the Tune, and thanks to Gaj and Kuhač, it is possible to contemplate one way in which the new song, originating from folk music, grew up: this Tune is a folkloric form, i.e. the—folklorism, because in 1833 it arises from the (supposed Polish) folklore, but at the same time, it also became—folklore.[9] Additionally, in parts of Slovenia, Croatia, Serbia and Montenegro, the Tune leads "a double life:" it neither stayed in the boundaries of Croatian tradition, nor was linked only to Gaj's lyrics.

Fig 2: Reveille, Croatia, Pjesmarica za pučke škole ... 1942: 137.

7 In one part of his book Stjepan Sremac deals with music and dance in the context of the Illyrian Movement, specifically emphasising the history of the *budnica* "Još Hrvatska ni propala." Sremac also cites the text of Franjo Ksaver Kuhač, who already in 1885 wrote that he suggested to Gaj that his inspiration for this song might have been a Polish song "Jesycye Polska nie zginela, polci my žijemi" (Sremac 2010: 62–63; http://www.karaoketexty.cz/texty-pisni/statni-hymny/polska-narodni-hymna-mayurek-d-browskiego-157454 (accessed 18 April 2012) and http://cs.wikipedia.org/wiki/Polská_hymna (accessed 18 April 2012).

8 Pettan received this information from his American mentor of Polish origin, ethnomusicologist and pianist Joseph Pacholczyk at the University of Maryland in Catonsville; Svanibor Pettan, personal communication with Zlata Marjanović, 27 October 2009.

9 A similar conclusion between folklorism and folklore could be found in Roginsky 2007: 41–66; about various aspects of folklorism see more in Ceribašić 2003.

Therefore, this Tune is trapped in the folklore of Slovenia, Croatia, Serbia and Montenegro.

In the first life, it represents a poetic and musical symbol of one nation, and exactly because of that, it is understandable, that it still stays connected to Croatian musical practice and the lyrics of Ljudevit Gaj. Therefore, the *budnica* became and stayed traditional, i.e. an equal and much respected part of Croatian musical practice (*Pjesmarica za pučke* ... 1942: 137).

According to the research of Croatian ethnomusicologist Joško Ćaleta, it is possible to find out that the above-mentioned *budnica* is a part of the repertoire of Croatian modern *klapa*[10] (Ćaleta 2008: 166), or on the Croatian Coast (Novi Vinodolski), where the Tune appears in carnival. The explanation of the aforementioned ethnomusicologist about the reasons of the practice of this *budnica* is that it was "most probably 'an answer' to the political situation in the country, because the lyrics "Još Hrvatska nij' propala" conclude what the state of their souls was (i.e. of those who perform it, authors comment), and where could you find a better situation to express that publicly than at a carnival?"[11]

TUNE'S "SECOND LIFE"

In its second life, the Tune becomes "released" from the lyrics, with which it arose, and lost its local (Croatian) identity. The Tune, also, becomes a melodic pattern.[12] On those grounds, in the musical traditions of Slovenia, Croatia, Serbia and Montenegro people create new vocal, vocal-instrumental or instrumental forms, in such way that despite of the undoubted recognisability of the Tune, they become local, traditional, and therefore become more authentic. In that way, this Tune, too, encourages both nation's performance and creativity.[13]

10 *Klapa*—a specific kind of group of singers from the Coastal-Mediterranean cultural area (see more in Marjanović 2011b: 437–438).

11 Joško Ćaleta, personal communication with Zlata Marjanović, 9 July 2009.

12 See more about the implementation of melodic patterns in the musical traditions of Croatia, Serbia, Montenegro, and during the past period in many other nations in Vasiljević 1964: 379, Petrović 1989: 82.

13 See more in Vasiljević 1964: 375.

Examples of that were, again, recorded on the Croatian territory, as well as in Slovenian and Serbian territory and in parts of the Montenegrin Seacoast.

In the above mentioned areas, the Tune "experiences" its transformation, since in the context of the various musical traditions of Slovenia, Croatia, Serbia and Montenegro it also adopts a new function. Therefore, this Tune represents a good example, first of the entire described occurrence of folklorism and yet a good example of a reverse process—disappearance of folklorism, i.e. how from that very folklorism, spontaneously arises different new forms of national musical practice.

According to the collected examples, the Tune "released" from Gaj's lyrics is most frequently linked to lyrics of a different genre. The ideas of followers of Romanticism from the second half of the 19th century influenced the occurrence of new songs. In accordance with that, the Tune most frequently "attracted" love poems, in the areas close to, or on the coasts of Adriatic Sea.[14] Very often, authors of those lyrics are known, but because of the features, the lyrics are accepted as folk (and names very soon become unknown).

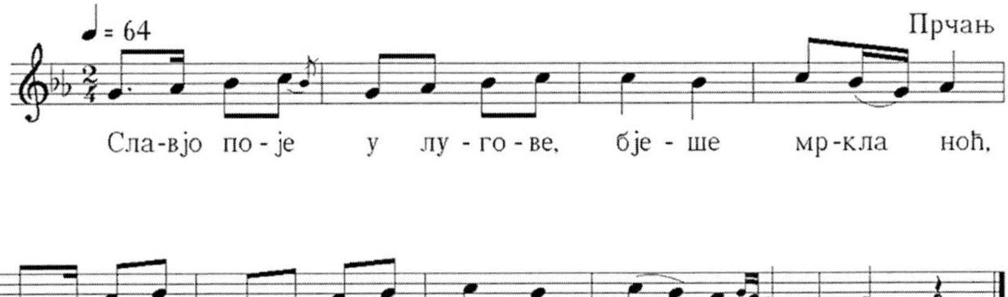

Fig. 3: Love song, Prčanj, Boka Kotorska Bay, Montenegro; Vasiljević 1965: No. 293.

So, in an Istrian village of Peroj (populated with Montenegrins), a love song "Ljubio se bjeli golub sa golubicom" was recorded (Vasiljević 1965: No.

14 Some of these lyrics, after having arisen, "travelled" and became connected with different tunes, from area to area (and can also be named patterns).

542),[15] whose lyrics were written in the "folk manner" in 1840 by a lawyer and poet, Jovan Subotić from Srem (1817–1886). During the national revival, in the second half of the 19th century, a maritime captain and poet Josip Jozo Đurović (1827–1883) from Boka Kotorska (Prčanj), made new, and again love lyrics for this Tune "Slavjo poje u lugove, bješe tamna noć" (Vasiljević 1965: No. 293, Luković 1951: 181).[16]

In Boka Kotorska, the Tune attached to love lyrics, whose authors stayed unknown. One of the songs was also recorded in Prčanj, and begins with the verse "Vrgom okom u dumbravi, zamjerih krune" (Vasiljević 1965: No. 293a), and the other was recorded in Bijela and begins with the "Ja uranih i podranih rano na vodu" (Vasiljević 1965: No. 202).

In Serbia, this Tune is performed with a tamboura ensemble and the lyrics "Poranila devojčica golube da hrani" (*Raspevana Vojvodina* 2003: No. 13), written by a poet Jovan Grčić Milenko (1846–1875) from Srem. As the author stressed, that is a "simple" text, that arose from a desire to "show" easily and directly in words the landscape and life generally, without affectation, or "fabricated" feelings (with a certain dose of realism, and even with signs of early Verism). The Tune of his song was changed to a certain degree, first of all because of the kind of verse, which comes from a thirteen-syllable verse, as noticeable in all other songs, and became a fourteen-syllable verse. In the mid-20th century, this Tune was also recorded with humorous lyrics in the small town of Ćićevac, in Serbia. There the mentioned Tune was altered, again because the verse has been added with one more syllable, so it becomes the fourteen-syllable verse (Vasiljević s.a.). At one moment and in some parts of the area studied the

15 How much these lyrics were popular can be proven by their connections to different tunes: during the 19th century in Slavonia and Serbia (Kuhač 1878: Nos. 309 and 310), in Perast (Sarno-San Giorgo 1896: No. 8), as well as during the 20th and 21st century in Morinj, Boka Kotorska Bay (Milinović 1974: No. 58), in Paštrovići, Montenegrin Coast (Marjanović 2002b), but also in Sandžak in Raška region (Vasiljević 1953b: No. 343) or mountain areas like Pešter-Sjenica in Raška region (Vukosavljević et al. 1984: No. 198).

16 See more about the lyrical variances of this song in Vasiljević 1965: Nos. 285, 328. See more about the wedding songs of Boka Kotorska Bay and Paštrovići, whose first verse was a part of the mentioned song, in Vasiljević 1965: Nos. 203, 279a.

Fig. 4: Humorous song, Ćićevac, Rasina district, Serbia; Vasiljević s.a.

Tune becomes a substitute for folklore, but also a keeper of ritual tradition that originated from rituals and customs (arising from a primeval need for survival). In Boka Kotorska Bay (Dobrota), it is possible to find the Tune as for Montenegrins it represents a very popular wedding song "Uz trpezu, niz trpezu, sivi sokole" (Vasiljević 1965: No. 238).[17]

Fig. 5: Ritual song, Gornja Lastva, Boka Kotorska Bay, Montenegro; Vasiljević 1965: No. 211.

17 The origin of these lyrics should certainly be looked for in beliefs connected to protective magic features of the falcon, with the folklore analogy between the bride and the falcon (see more in Ajdačić 1998: 228).

In Boka Kotorska Bay (Gornja Lastva) the Tune was sung with the text "Paun pase, trava raste, pauniću moj" as a vocal and dance form (Vasiljević 1965: No. 211).[18]

Tellers of Boka Kotorska Bay (Prčanj) deem that the Tune was used at weddings and as women's songs (*ženske pjesme*), i.e. the ritual songs performed by women. In time, this song became desacralised (i.e. from a ritual, it turned into a love song), and it stopped being just a part of Prčanj tradition. It experienced this transformation in the second half of the 20th century, when it got its place in the *klapa* repertoire (which is typical for Dalmatian multipart group singing, Gregović 2006: 33).[19]

In Slovenia, there is a song "Našla sem jo, našla sem jo, zlato jabolko," which is sung to the Tune, which also could have ritual origins:[20] 'I found, I found a gold apple / I gave it, I gave it to my father to share. // Father does not know, Father does not know the right to share, / He gave more to himself then me …'[21] Further the song lists the other members of the family, at the end she gives the apple to the boy (her future husband?), who knows how to share properly.[22]

In life and in nature, one can spot certain circular processes that have not passed over the Tune's life either. The same as during the Tune's arising, and despite the numerous listed genre varieties, in practice it is still connected to patriotic lyrics. Therefore, in the Tune's example one can see a universal hu-

18 See more about the ritual-magical and possibly totemic origin of this dance and singing in Mladenović 1973: 117.

19 The song in question was processed for Dalmatian multipart singing group by Nikola Gregović from Kotor (Boka Kotorska, Gregović 2006: 33).

20 Mirko Ramovš and Rebeka Kunej, personal communication with Zlata Marjanović, 25 September 2009.

21 Našla sem jo, našla sem jo, zlato jabolko, / dala sem jo, dala sem jo ocu talati. // Oče ne zna, oče ne zna pravo talati, / sebi više, sebi više nego meni da …

22 This text is very reminiscent of a wedding text "Crveno cvjeće cvjetaše" (Red Flowers bloomed) sung in some parts of the Montenegrian Hinterland and Croatian Seacoast: flowers gathered by the future bride, she gave flowers to all members of her household, but no one will take these, except her future husband (see more in Marjanović Krstić 1998: No. 133, Marjanović 2005a: Nos. 222–226, Bonifačić Rožin 1964–65: 43 etc.).

or. in As-dur

Fig. 6: Ritual song, Kotor, Boka Kotorska Bay, Montenegro; Klapa Karampana ... 2009.

man need for praise, not only in Croatia, but also in coastal parts of Montenegro. In the town of Budva and in a smaller place Bijela (Boka Kotorska Bay) it is in practice the song “Polećela dva anđela, oba sa neba.” This patriotic song was dedicated to historical persons who were important for Montenegrins, and especially to King Nikola I.[23]

23 The proverbial patriotism of Montenegrins was demonstrated by the lyrics of this song, that mention not only about persons from an older period of history (Beg Ivan I, Tzar Dušan), but also about the Montenegrin Prince and King Nikola Petrović Njegoš (1841–1921). King Nikola I was not just a politician, but also an artist. His literature was inspired by patriotism and praise for the heroic battle of the Montenegrin nation (especially prominent is the drama “Balkanska carica” (The Balkans Empress) and the epic “Pesnik i vila” (A Poet and a Fairy); see more in Šentija 1980: 26.

Fig. 7: Patriotic song, Bijela, Boka Kotorska Bay, Montenegro; Marjanović Krstić 1998: No. 86.

According to the singers of Bijela, they learnt this song by heart, during their childhood from their fathers, in the first half of the 20th century and it is considered as a part of their tradition. They also consider that the lyrics date from around 1900 in Boka Kotorska Bay, but they do not know the author's name. The mentioned song is being performed during various folk gatherings in parts of Boka Kotorska Bay (for example, in parts of wedding ceremonies, when the bride has already been brought to her new home), as well as during the more important church ceremonies, and therefore it got the status of an unofficial church anthem (Marjanović 1996: 86).[24]

In addition to those listed sound recordings and musical transcriptions of vocal and vocal-instrumental practice, the Tune was also recorded as a part of instrumental practice. For example, at the end of the 19th century Franjo Ksaver Kuhač transcribed a dance "Krivka" in Banat (Kuhač 1880: No. 1176).

One such example was noticed among the population of Pregrada (Krapina) as well, in a tamboura performance "Svirka," as a B-part, where the mentioned Tune was used (*Hrvatska tradicijska kultura* 2004: No. 29). That was done in Slovenia also. In the dance called "Trojka" the Tune was performed with the following instruments: a grand cymbal, a violin, a viola, a flute and a small double bass (*Zvočnost slovenskih pokrajin* 1991:

24 In the first half of the 20th century in Budva (Montenegro Seacoast) a master-shoemaker lived and worked from whom Petar Jelušić learned to sing. Petar often sang this song to his master, because the master regularly paid all singers who would sing this song.

Fig. 8: "Krivka" dance, Banat, Vojvodina, Serbia; Kuhač 1880: No. 1176.

No. 6).[25] At the same time, in parts of Slovenia the "Trojka" was often performed as a dance in the repertoire of folklore groups (Ramovš: 1996).[26]

Due to nostalgia in urbanised environments for some lost "roots," or "nature," the Tune has its varieties which emerged from ideological and commercial initiatives of the modern culture. An example for this is an advertisement on the Croatian National Broadcast Network that was broadcasted at the end of April 2009 (which confirmed how obvious the respect

25 Slovenian ethnomusicologists believed that "Trojka" emerged in Slovenia after the First World War and was transferred by the tamboura ensembles (Ramovš: 1996). See more about the dance "Trojka" in Slovenia in Ramovš 1996: 39–43, 1997: 42–57.

26 Mirko Ramovš, personal communication with Zlata Marjanović, 25 September 2009.

for the Tune was in Croatia). There, the Tune was used as the music cover for Karlovac beer, which was said to be used traditionally since the 19th century (i.e. from the time of Ljudevit Gaj and Ferdo Livadić).

Fig. 9: "Trojka" dance, Hotiza, Prekmurje, Slovenia; Ramovš 1996: No. 6.

CONCLUSION

After everything that has been discussed, there is a need to explain the popularity of the Tune in Slovenia, Croatia, Serbia and Montenegro. There are several different starting points:

1. Considering the most important musical features of the Tune. It is clear, simple, rounded with a period, singable, cheerful, easy to remember, and self-sufficient. Singers give similar observations: "The Tune of this song is pretty singable, melodic" (Bijela, Boka Kotorska Bay). For that reason, it certainly has a character of a starting melo-rhythmic pattern (interval of major third), which is obviously, easily sealed into musical consciousness with its repetitions (in the second bar completely, in the third bar in a tone lower etc.). If one implements the conclusions from the literature on this repetition principle, according to which that is one of significant archetypal musical thinking, there is a reason for the wider implementation and favouritism of the Tune in the music tradition of Slovenia, Croatia, Serbia

and Montenegro.[27] The Tune's rhythm is also clear, syllabic and vigorous, it dominates, undoubtedly attracts and organizes, and unites those who listen to it or perform it (as ethnomusicologist Miodrag Vasiljević emphasizes, the rhythm arose from movement, it expresses the rhythm, it is performed through movement, initiates us to move, it is spotted through movement).[28] This is a rhythm very close to a march, and perhaps it is not randomly chosen, if one pays attention to Gaj's wish to express his patriotic words with the music, in the best way for that purpose, adequate rhythm could gather and incite the like-minded.[29] In any way, he was attracted and inspired by the part, played by some village "double bass" (an instrument which in the first place has a harmonic-rhythmic role in an ensemble), and in a *budnica*'s musical transcription it is stressed that the *budnica* should be performed as if it was "a march."[30] If, at the end, such a Tune would be "placed" in some of the lower voices of the polyphonic composition, it could be understood as ostinato, because as a remarkable impulse, it undoubtedly initiated many, not just musical processes in the tradition of Slovenia, Croatia, Serbia and Montenegro.

2. The Tune, after having arisen, was written down in 1833. That action accomplished a guarantee of repetition and wider implementation, not just of *budnica*, but also of the Tune, and thereby gave less possibility to forget it.

27 See more about the repetition principle, as one of the archetypal ways of thinking in Jakovljević 2008: 10–14 and Marjanović 2008b: 111.

28 See more in Vasiljević 1953a: XX and XXI.

29 From the aspect of the type of verse, Gaj used thirteen-syllable verses, with two caesuras, which continued to occur in the majority of lyrics that in the end are connected with the Tune. But, that is a common verse in literature and in musical tradition (especially those of rural style and ritual origin) of many nations in the area observed (see more in Ružić 1992: 880, Latković 1981: 148, Simić 1968: 255, Marjanović Krstić 1998: 42).

30 The cited rhythmic features are also closely connected to harmonic features of the Tune (the musical component, which in terms of Western European classical music are not familiar in rural areas in the musical tradition of Croatia, Serbia and Montenegro; about tonal bases and harmonic features of the rural musical tradition in Serbia, for example, see more in Jović Miletić 2011: 32–71). That way, the sequence of basic harmonic functions, of Western European classical music (from tonic to dominant and vice versa from dominant to tonic), which also gets the features of a march in the Tune rhythm, can clearly be recognised ("heard").

Confirmation by the citations represents other, plentiful musical transcriptions and sound recordings of the Tune, listed at the beginning of this work, without which this work would not have existed.

3. Reconsideration of the Tune in the context of cultural exchange. The origination of the Tune from 1833 and further covering of an area (i.e. in Slovenia, Croatia, Serbia, Montenegro) could also be seen as acceptance of some influences from Western European classical music.[31] The Tune does not become a part of tradition of the continental-mountainous cultural area,[32] because it is completely different.[33] The area at which it stays and survives should be at least a bit urbanised.

In that way it can primarily be noticed in the lyrics that were added to the Tune in urban or urbanised settlements (of Vojvodina, and Boka Kotorska Bay).[34] Probably, that is a way the song from Ćićevac (as an urbanised settlement) is different: due to the conflict between an old-fashioned rural

31 Some of the features of these influences are rhymed lyrics organised in verses, a tune based on major tonality, homophonic two-part or multipart performances etc.

32 Research of ecclesiastical Serbian heritage, for example, show that while in the newly arisen urban areas of the Danube River Basin, social process was growing under Western European classical music influence (see more about the waking of national conscience during the 19th century in the musical tradition of Serbia and Montenegro: Pejović 2006: 5–30, Vlahović 1983: 51–94 etc.), but in the inner part of the Balkans there was still a rural musical style in the continental-mountainous cultural area. The continental-mountainous cultural area subsumes the culture of the continental and rural parts of Montenegro, Herzegovina and Dalmatian Hinterland (where the so-called patriarchal social system exists; see more in Cvijić 1991: 335–404).

33 Some of the features of the musical tradition of the continental-mountainous cultural area are the use of melodic models for performing various lyrics, tunes are of limited range, mostly of several tones, the sonority between the tones is mostly less then a tempered semi-tone etc. (about musical tradition in rural parts of Montenegro see more in Vasiljević 1965, or, for example, Boka Kotorska Bay, or parts of Montenegrin Coast with its Hinterland in Marjanović Krstić 1998, Marjanović 2005a, Marjanović 2005b, Marjanović 2008b, Marjanović 2011a: 129, 130 etc.).

34 The term urbanised settlements considers smaller places, that do not have a city structure, but where the cultural way of living is closer to the town way, than to the village way of living. Having that in mind, places with such structure are less isolated than the rural places.

way of thinking and a new urban music "trend," the neutral territory was used, i.e. humorous lyrics were shaped into a fourteen-syllable verse (instead of the lyrics of ritual origin and thirteen-syllable verse).

Confirmation of musical influences from the Western European classical music, as well as the individual features of musical tradition of Slovenia, Croatia, Serbia and Montenegro, can all clearly be considered through the musical form of the chosen examples. Where this process made a stronger influence, peculiar two-part forms can be noticed. Therefore, the Tune always occurs as a B-part. Prior to it, there is an A-part, which is always, in "the manner" of the Tune itself, but from examples, in terms of music, it is different (performance from Pregrada, *Hrvatska tradicijska kultura* 2004: No. 29). It also happens that the Tune is in C major, but its first part is in a parallel, a minor ("Krivka," Kuhač 1880: No. 1176). In some examples, there is an introductory improvisation prior to the Tune, which is partially preconditioned with features of the instrument with which it is being played; e.g. a grand cymbal in "Trojka" in Prekmurje, Slovenia (*Zvočnost slovenskih pokrajin* 1991: No. 6). Sometimes, a song whose lyrics are ritual, such as a song recorded in Boka Kotorska Bay starts with the Tune (A-part), to which is added its second, different musical B-part in the form of a refrain (ibid.). In contrast to the exposed, in areas where a rural way of playing is represented, examples are based on the Tune, without connecting it with other, different music materials (see examples "Slavjo poje u lugove, bješe mrkla noć" in Vasiljević 1965: 293, "Ja uranih i podranih rano na vodu" in Vasiljević 1965: 202, "Neko voli seljančicu, neko gospođicu" in Vasiljević, and "Polećela dva anđela oba sa neba" in Marjanović 1996: 86).

This Tune arrived as folklorism but it became a part of folklore. In the author's opinion, this is because each nation has accepted the Tune as "their own" and because each nation is identified through the Tune. In short, in the musical tradition of Slovenia, Croatia, Serbia and Montenegro the Tune is trapped in folklore and it is almost certain that the current year 2012 is just another one in the line of its practice. It seems that the Tune "found" Ljudevit Gaj, not vice versa, and it found him thanks to its musical features, and after that it created its widespread "field" (both in time and territory), and was almost entirely anticipated with one strophe of Gaj's reveille: 'Faithful people of old glory, / From Lika, Krbava. // Carnolians, Styrians, Gorotans, / and Slavonia, / Bosnia, Serbs, Istrians, / and Dalmatia' (Kuhač 1881: 362).[35]

35 Stare slave vjerni svati, / z Like, Krbave. // Kranjci, Štajer, Gorotanci / i Slavonija / Bosna, Srbi, Istrijanci, / ter Dalmacija …

REFERENCES

Ajdačić, Dejan
1998 Žanrovi svadbenih pesama. *Kodovi slovenskih kultura* 3 – svadba: 218–238.

Andreis, Josip
1966 *Historija muzike.* Prvi svezak. Zagreb: Školska knjiga.

Ansambel Trutamora Slovenica
2011 Ansambel Trutamora Slovenica iz Ljubljane, Dobitnik priznanja ACS 2000 http://www.youtube.com/watch?v=Qjht-sBiKeU (accessed 13 May 2012).

Bonifačić Rožin, Nikola
1964–65 Svadbena dramatika u Dubrovačkom primorju. *Narodna umjetnost* 3: 39–73.

Ceribašić, Naila
2003 *Hrvatsko, seljačko, starinsko i domaće: povijest i etnografija javne prakse narodne glazbe u Hrvatskoj.* Zagreb: Institut za etnologiju i folkloristiku.

Cvijić, Jovan
1991 *Balkansko poluostrvo.* Beograd: Srpska akademija nauka i umetnosti Beograd, Zavod za udžbenike i nastavna sredstva Beograd, Novinsko-izdavačka radna organizacija "Književnje novine" Beograd.

Cvetko, Dragotin
1960 *Zgodovina glasbene umetnosti na Slovenskem III.* Ljubljana: Državna založba Slovenije.

Ćaleta, Joško
2008 Modern Klapa Movement – Multipart Singing as a Popular Tradition. In: Ahmedaja, Ardian, and Gerlinde Haid (eds.), *European Voices I, Multipart Singing in the Balkan and the Mediterranean.* Wien: Böhlau Verlag, 159–176.

Dvorniković, Vladimir
2000 *Karakterologija Jugoslovena.* Beograd: Prosveta, fototipsko izdanje.

Gregović, Nikola
2006 *Antologija klapskih pjesama.* Kotor: self-published.

Hrvatska tradicijska kultura
2004 *Hrvatska tradicijska kultura.* Zagreb: Institut za etnologiju i fokloristiku. (DVD)

Jakovljević, Rastko
2008 Encoding the Archetype: The Cases of Rapetition and Contrast in Music. In: Janeliauskas, Rimantas (ed.), *Proceesing of scientific gathering Muzikos kompanavimo principai: muzikos archetipai,* 8-oji tarptautine muzikos teorijos konferencija, Vilnius, April 23 - 25. Vilnius: Lithuanian Academy of Music and Theatre, Lithuanian Composers' Union, 10–17.

Jović Miletić, Aleksandra
2011 *Početno muzičko obrazovanje na srpskom muzičkom jeziku.* Beograd: Dijamant print.

Klapa Karampana ...
2009 Klapa Karampana – Paun leti n[videspot]. http://www.youtube.com/watch?v=nh0xvdpvOlU (accessed 21 January 2009).

Kuhač, Franjo Ksaver
1880 *Južno-slovjenske narodne popievke.* III knjiga. Zagreb: Tiskara i litografija C. Albrechta.
1881 *Južno-slovjenske narodne popievke.* IV knjiga. Zagreb: Tiskara i litografija C. Albrechta.

Latković, Vido
1982 *Narodna književnost 1.* Beograd: Naučna knjiga.

Luković, Niko
1951 *Boka Kotorska.* Cetinje: Narodna knjiga.

Marjanović, Zlata
1996 *Narodna muzika Boke Kotorske.* Unpublished manuscript.

2002a *Narodna muzika Budve.* Unpublished manuscript.

2002b *Narodna muzika Paštrovića.* Unpublished manuscript.

2005a *Narodna muzilka Grblja.* Novi Sad: Društvo za obnovu manastira Podlastva, Grbalj, Kotor, Boka Kotorska, Institut za muzikologiju i etnomuzikologiju Crne Gore, Podgorica.

2005b Primorju na veliko znamenje. Prilog proučavanju muzičke tradicije Crnogorskog primorja. In: Đurašković, Lucija (ed.), *Zbornik radova sa simpozijuma 'Stefan Mitrov Ljubiša u kontekstu mediteranske kulture' održanog u Budvi 27. i 28. februara 2002. godine.* Budva: Javna Ustanova "Muzeji galerija i biblioteka" Budva, Muzeji - Spomen dom "Stefan Mitrov Ljubiša", 245–283.

2008a Kontinuitet i razvoj muzičke tradicije Crnogorskog primorja sa zaledjem (na primeru grbaljskog pevanja, ali i Miodrag Vasiljević je ipak bio u Grblju!). In: Golemović, Dimitrije O. (ed.), *Zbornik radova sa naučnog skupa "Dani Vlade S. Miloševića."* Banja Luka: Akademija nauka i umjetnosti Banja Luka, Muzikološko društvo Republike Srpske, 179–196.

2008b Full Voice Songs in Montenegro Seacoast with Hinterland. In: Janeliauskas, Rimantas (ed.), *Proceesing of scientific gathering Muzikos kompanavimo principai: muzikos archetipai*, 8-oji tarptautine muzikos teorijos konferencija, Vilnius, April 23 - 25, 2008. Vilnius: Lithuanian Academy of Music and Theatre, Luthuanian Composers' Union, 110–115.

2011a Cultural listening in multipart traditional singing on the Northern and Central Montenegro Coast and its hinterland. In: Ahmedaja, Ardian (ed.), *European Voices II. Cultural listening and Local Discourse in Multipart Singing Tradition in Europe.* Wien, Köln, Weimar: Böhlau Verlag, 127–139.

2011b Lexicon of local terminology on multipart singing: Montenegro seacoast with hinterland. In: Ahmedaja, Ardian (ed.), *European Voices II. Cultural listening and Local Discourse in Multipart Singing Tradition in Europe.* Wien, Köln, Weimar: Böhlau Verlag, 435–448.

Marjanović Krstić, Zlata
1998 *Vokalna muzička tradicija Boke Kotorske.* Podgorica: Udruženje kompozitora Crne Gore.

Milinović, Špiro
1974 *Podaci o istoriji Morinja i okolnih mjesta.* Kotor: Turističko društvo "Morinj."

Mladenović, Olivera
1973 *Kolo u Južnih Slovena.* Beograd: Srpska akademija nauka i umetnosti, Etnografski institut.

Pejović, Roksanda
2006 Rađanje srpske solo pesme. In: Perković Radak, Ivana et al. (eds.), *Istorija i misterija muzike u čast Roksande Pejović.* Beograd: Fakultet muzičke umetnosti, 5–30.

Petrović, Radmila
1989 *Srpska narodna muzika – pesma kao izraz narodnog muzičkog mišljenja.* Posebna izdanja, knjiga DXCIII, Odeljenje društvenih nauka, knj. 98. Beograd: Srpska akademija nauka i umetnosti.

Pjesmarica za pučke škole ...
1942 *Pjesmarica za pučke škole – izdanje za učitelje.* Zagreb: Nezavisna država Hrvatska.

Raspevana Vojvodina
2003 *Raspevana Vojvodina.* Anđelka Govedarović i Tamburaški orkestar Radio Televizije Novi Sad. Beograd: Radio televizija Srbije, Produkcija gramofonskih ploča. (CD)

Ramovš, Mirko
1996 *Polka je ukazana. Plesno izročilo na Slovenskem. Prekmurje in Porabje.* Ljubljana: Založba Kres.
1997 *Polka je ukazana. Plesno izročilo na Slovenskem. Vzhodna Štajerska.* Ljubljana: Založba Kres.

Roginsky, Dina
2007 Folklore, Folklorism, and Synchronization: Preserved-Created Folklore in Israel. *Journal of Folklore Research* 44 (1): 41–66.

Ružić, Žarko
1992 Trinaesterac. In: [s.n.], *Rečnik književnih termina.* Beograd: Nolit, 880–881.

Sarno-San Giorgo, Dionisio de
1896 *Uspomena iz Perasta. Narodne pjesme za pevanje i klavir.* Beograd: Izdanje D. M. Gjorića.

Simić, Ljuba
1968 Nekoji arhaični elementi u svatovskim pesmama Bosne i Hercegovine. In: Kumer, Zmaga (ed.), *Zbornik XII kongresa jugoslovanskih folkloristov,* Celje 1965. Ljubljana: ZDFJ, 249–256.

Sremac, Stjepan
2010 *Povijest i praksa scenske primjene folklornog plesa u Hrvata.* Zagreb: Institut za etnologiju i folkloristiku.

Stepanov, Stepan
1956 Narodne popijevke kotara Gospić, god. 1956. ZIF rkp. zbirka N 225.

Šentija, Josip (ed.)
1980 *Opća enciklopedija.* Volume 6. Zagreb: Jugoslovenski leksikografski zavod.

Tomc, Matija
1948 *Igraj kolce! Za mladinski zbor.* Ljubljana: Državna založba Slovenije.

Vasiljević, Miodrag
1953a *Jugoslovenski muzički folklor II. Narodne melodije koje se pevaju u Makedoniji.* Beograd: Prosveta.

1953b *Narodne melodije Sandžaka.* Beograd: Srpska akademija nauka i umetnosti, Muzikološki institut.

1956 *Narodne melodije Crne Gore.* Posebna izdanja, knj. 12. Beograd: Srpska akademija nauka i umetnosti, Muzikološki institut.

1964 Funkcije i vrste glasova u srpskom narodnom pevanju. In: [s.n.], *Zbornik radova VII kongresa folklorista Jugoslavije*. Ohrid: [Savez folklorista Jugoslavije], 375–380.

s.a. Unpublished music transcriptions from Rasina district. Phonoarchive of the Department of Ethnomusicology of music school Stevan Mokranjac of Kraljevo, Serbia.

Vukosavljević, Petar, et al.

1984 *Narodne melodije, igre i nošnje Peštersko-sjeničke visoravni*. Beograd: Radio-Beograd.

Zvočnost slovenskih pokrajin

1991 *Zvočnost slovenskih pokrajin*. 4. Ljubljana: self-published. (CD)

Rebeka Kunej

LOOKING AT FOLK DANCE: THE OVERLOOKED RESOURCES OF OLD GRAMOPHONE RECORDS

ABSTRACT

The article aims to analyse the reasons for the neglect of old gramophone records and their content as a scientific resource in ethnochoreology research in Slovenia. It uses the case of a specific music group and their discography to present the contribution of old commercial gramophone records to the understanding and research of Slovenian folk dance.

Key words: dance research, Slovenian folk dance, gramophone records, historical resource

INTRODUCTION

Ethnochoreology research in Slovenia has been marked by researchers only focusing on elements of dance tradition which had begun to decline or was remembered only by a handful of individuals by the time the research took place. Although the researchers were mainly interested in folk dance as a choreologic form, they were also concerned with the accompanying instrumental music. At the same time the predominant belief was that folk dance and the accompanying music are unique and that folk dance music and its characteristics can only be found by doing field research, with audio recordings being vital for the research. As a result, other audio recordings, such as gramophone records, were completely ignored as a comparative resource in ethnochoreology research. The aim of this paper is to determine why gramophone records have not been considered as a scientific resource in ethnochoreology research in Slovenia. Old gramophone records significantly contribute to the understanding of the folk music of their time, especially instrumental folk dance music, as well as its sound imagery. I intend to support my thesis using the gramophone records recorded by the Hoyer Trio.

THE RESEARCH OF FOLK DANCE AND THE FOLK DANCE MUSIC IN SLOVENIA

Slovenian ethnochoreologist Mirko Ramovš[1] used the term folk dance to define those dances "which are typical of the broadest population groups. They derive from the tradition which could have been either inherited from ancient times, where the time cannot be fully defined today, or they had been purposely adopted from somewhere at a certain time and then continued to spread intermittently" (Ramovš 1992: 7). The author then narrowed down this broad definition of Slovenian folk dances to those dances or dance traditions which were maintained by rural inhabitants of the Slovenian ethnic territory up to the years before World War II. Thus research interest in folk dance was limited by their social context and the perspective of time. However, later in one of his last definitions, Ramovš defined folk dances as "social dances, which in Slovenia survived in the countryside until World War II, and in certain places they continue to persist, mostly among the rural people, while some of the dances (the waltz, the polka, the mazurka) were also danced in the cities" (Ramovš 2005: 89).

Therefore, ethnochoreology research was focused more on the rural inhabitants and less on other social classes of the Slovenian population, arguing that the majority of the Slovenian population until World War II belonged to the peasantry. Such narrow focus was partly the result of the research preferences of individuals (Ramovš 1992: 7). The image of folk-dance tradition in Slovenia and knowledge of these dances is based on the

1 The leading ethnochoreologist of the late 20th century Mirko Ramovš, my predecessor, had researched folk dance from the time of his employment at the Institute of Ethnomusicology at the Scientific Research Centre of the Slovenian Academy of Sciences and Arts in 1966 until his retirement in 2003. His written descriptions and labanotations scores that represent the majority of the existing transcriptions of folk dance from the entire Slovenian ethnic territory, also created a systematically organised catalog of them. His numerous scholarly discussions on the origin, development and characteristics of individual folk dances mostly appeared in the journal *Traditiones*. He published a representative selection of dances in his monograph *Plesat me pelji* (Take me dancing; 1980) and a collection of folk dances in seven books with a common title *Polka je ukazana. Plesno izročilo na Slovenskem* (A polka is ordered. Dance tradition in Slovenia; 1992–2000).

field research of a handful of researchers who conducted their research mostly in the second half of the 20th century. Consequently, their research created an image of folk dance that was limited to the end of the 19th century and the first half of the 20th century.

Slovenian folkloristics has included the research of folk dance and instrumental folk music, predominantly music for dancing, among its research projects, which started when the Folklore Institute was established after the institutionalisation of folklore research in 1934 (today the Institute of Ethnomusicology at the Scientific Research Centre of the Slovenian Academy of Sciences and Arts). An important milestone was reached after World War II, when the Institute increased the numbers of its employees as well as developing technically, acquiring the equipment which was finally capable of capturing the sonority of the "disappearing" Slovenian folk dance music in the field. In 1954 the Institute acquired two tape recorders (cf. Kunej 1999). Thus 1955 saw the beginnings of the field recording of folk dance music and the development of an extensive sound archive. It was understood until recently that the oldest audio examples of Slovenian folk dance music are directly connected with the field research of the Institute of Ethnomusicology and its tape recordings. I am not inclined to directly agree with this statement, for after listening to the old gramophone records I found audio examples that could be determined as folk music.

The researchers whose research subject focused on folk dance music tended to concentrate on their own field research. Initially that included writing down the score of dance tunes and later also recording the music on a tape recorder. The founder of the Institute France Marolt[2] did use gramophone records in his research, mainly in the presentation of the vocal music, however in a different manner and with a different intention. In 1936 he started with a series of radio broadcasts called "Slovenian Folk Song," which were broadcast by Radio Ljubljana. In this series of radio lectures Marolt also included audio examples of typical folk songs, often in his own arrange-

2 France Marolt (1891–1951) was the initiator and founder of the Folklore Institute. He was also known as a choir master and founder of the *Akademski pevski zbor* (Academic Choir, 1926), for which he arranged Slovenian folk songs.

ment and performed by vocal groups he himself led, which had been previously recorded on gramophone records (so-called direct cut records). Consequently, a small collection of gramophone records developed from 1936 onward, which represented Slovenian folk music, although in most cases we can talk about "enriched" versions of the original folk music. Despite his specific usage of gramophone records in his applied ethnomusicological approach, neither Marolt, nor his successive researchers, considered commercial gramophone records or their contents to be a relevant source for the research of folk music heritage.

Today the gramophone records are linked to the terms popular (mass) culture and commercial music production. Quite possibly it was not much different in the past. I consider the association of the gramophone records with these two terms to be the reason that the records were not included in the past ethnochoreology research, not even as a material for comparative research, despite the fact that part of the music on the gramophone records can be placed in the same time frame and/or geographic area being researched. Moreover, some of the records were recorded in the United States of America, which could have prompted an additional negative attitude toward the recorded audio material. An example of such negative views of the audio recordings done in America can be seen on the first page of the weekly magazine *Radio Ljubljana*, which features a discussion on the Slovenian music on the radio. According to an unknown author the issue lies in the problem of Slovenian records; in 1933 there was no record production in Slovenia, therefore the radio programme depended on foreign record production. Later in the article he says: "So whatever is the cheapest for the foreign company and whatever 'sells' best is then recorded. And it is clear that first-rate things are not cheap and that what 'sells' is bad ('kitsch') rather than good." (*Vprašanje* ... 1933: 193). He then continues by saying that people get upset by the singing of some, laugh at the singing of others and are appalled by the diction of the third. He notes that although some are upset because of the numerous cases like that, a vast group of people enjoy the whole affair. The author concludes his review by saying: "Singing for the gramophone cannot serve as merely a lovely way to earn money for those we hardly know of at home. Slovenian records should preserve the beauty of our song for later generations and convey this to the vast numbers of foreigners, having been performed by our best" (*Vprašanje* … 1933: 193). Although the author remains unknown, I believe that France Marolt could have also written these words, especially when considering that in his quest he often and without prejudice corrected folk music. Furthermore, he later began to co-operate with Radio Ljubljana.

SLOVENIANS IN AMERICA AS FOREIGN SPEAKING CUSTOMERS

78 rpm gramophone records were characteristic for commercial music production in the first half of the 20th century. The crisis in the sales of gramophone records in the 1920's and early 1930's, brought about by the rise of the radio, and the subsequent struggle produced a valuable heritage for Slovenians.

One of the strategies used to attract buyers of gramophones and gramophone records in the States was to record music for the so-called foreign speaking customers in America. Agents of different gramophone companies scouted among the immigrants in New York and elsewhere in search for performers to record music in their mother tongue. First, they recorded national anthems and other well-known songs from Europe (accompanied by a studio orchestra), later they added recordings of popular and folk songs and musicians playing typical folk instruments.

Slovenians were not exempt from this. The first recordings of Slovenian music in the United States were made before World War I. Those of the soprano Augusta Danilova, the duet of Augusta Danilova and Mila Polančeva and the Slovenian choir society *Slavec* can be found among the earliest and best known recordings. These were usually well-known folk songs accompanied by an accordion or a smaller instrumental group. Only a few years later the first dance tunes were recorded. The recordings of Matt Hoyer or the Hoyer Trio, which I discuss below, were not the first gramophone recordings of Slovenian instrumental dance music[3]. However, they undoubtedly play an important role in the image of recorded dance music at that specific time in the history of gramophone records, as their music practice importantly contributed to creating the Slovenian space in America during the 1920's.

THE HOYER TRIO

Matija Arko, in the United States known as Matt Hoyer[4] was born in 1891 in Sodražica near Ribnica in the Dolenjska region in Slovenia. In 1911 he emmigrated to Cleveland, USA. He died in 1961 in New York. He was the founder and leader of the Hoyer Trio, one of the first well-known groups in the States which included the diatonic accordion and was thus one of the pioneers of the Cleveland style polka groups. Matija Arko borrowed his family name Hojer for his stage name, under which he was known. Different musicians played in the trio, mostly Frank and Ed Simončič and Frank Novak (Terselic and Debevec 2009: 197). They usually played a guitar and a banjo, sometimes even a second accordion as accompaniment. The typical arrangement of the group combined traditional Slovenian in-

3 Thus a group called *Slovenska kmečka godba* (Slovenian peasant band) in Ljubljana often recorded for the gramophone companies Favorite and Gramophone Co. between 1908 and 1910 (cf. Kunej 2012). The titles include dances which can undoubtedly be placed among the Slovenian folk dances: *mazurka*, *star kmečki ples*, *marzolin*, *mazurka na poskok*, *domači tramplan*, *krajc-polka*, and a number of polkas and waltzes. Among the newspaper advertisements for gramophone records of the period we can find individual titles which are classified as folk-dance music: e.g. *praštajerc*, *galop*, *sotiš*, *lendler*, recorded also by other groups, mostly brass bands.

4 In the article I use the American version of his name because he had been better known and respected in the United States than in his home country. As can be seen from my own ethnological research in his home village or region, he has been all but forgotten. Despite his relative importance and his defining influence, he represented the popular worldwide music trend in the 1920's, he is completely overlooked and forgotten in his home country (he cannot be found in the *Slovenian biographical lexicon*, finding his birthplace was also an issue as the local people are not aware of him). I would also like to point out that in the written material (newspapers) and on gramophone record labels he can be found under different names or surnames: Matt, Matija and Hoyer, Hojer or even Arko as well as a variety of combinations of these names and surnames.

struments with those which were quite rare in Slovenia at that time; we can actually say they were not used in the Slovenian environment. Although the way of playing remains fairly similar to that which could be defined as a folk in dance music in Slovenia at the time, the arrangement which includes a diatonic accordion and a banjo is a "winning" Slovenian-American combination. Matt Hoyer and his Trio contributed significantly to the Slovenian space in America of the 1920's as well as to the rise of the Cleveland style polka music, with which Slovenian immigrants in America as well as others were able to identify.

Their biggest bestseller was a polka called *Dunaj ostane Dunaj* (Vienna Forever), which is actually an Austrian march. Interestingly, this tune is known today as the *Hoyer's Polka* among the fans of the Cleveland style polka music. In addition, their most popular compositions in the United States include mostly polkas—*Jack on St. Clair Polka*, *Bartender's Polka*, *Zip Polka*, and a host of others (*The National* ... s.a.).

The Hoyer Trio was a very popular Slovenian group in the United States. This is obvious from the number of issued gramophone records as well as articles from newspapers of the Slovenian immigrants in America (*Ameriška domovina*, *Glasilo K.s.K jednote*). This can be seen from the announcements of events from the 1920's and 1930's, which included the Hoyer Trio, who would play music for dancing. The amount of recorded material of Matt Hoyer and his Trio is enviable, especially when we take into account that the group recorded with Columbia, Victor and OKeh in the short period of five years. Consequently the "entire" production of gramophone records, which are the subject of the following analysis, took place in the period of 1924–1929. According to the data known so far (cf. Kunej 2008: 195–199) their output includes 68 independent recordings from the Trio and 21 recordings of the Trio or Matt Hoyer in collaboration with singers or other musicians.

As it was common in the industry of gramophone records of the time, some of the recordings of the Hoyer Trio which also fit other target groups were re-issued on gramophone records and renamed in the language of the target groups. The same recording, the identity of which can be determined with the matrix number printed on the record, thus got a completely different title or was translated. Consequently *Ven pa not – polka* was renamed into the *Regina Polka* or *Jen vesele – polka*, the recording of *Slovenska polka* (Slovenian Polka) became the *Warsaw Polka*, *Knäpparpolka* or *Vstuvity – Polka. Primorski valček* (The Primorska Waltz) was also sold under three different names: *Amore Campagniolo – valzer*, *Siwe Oczy – walc* and *Gammal Vastgötavals*. In his monograph Drago Kunej (2008: 199–200) specifies ten such recordings which were given up to three different names in foreign languages. The polka and waltz rhythms of all ten recordings of the Hoyer Trio appealed to different foreign areas. Although Slovenian folk dance belongs to the larger middle European territory, from the perspective of choreography it can be more closely linked to the dance forms of the German language area. The tunes which were not polkas or waltzes were not presented to the other target groups in such a way. Therefore we can say that, unlike other folk dances, the polka and the waltz in that time were two important dance forms in the larger American-European areas of music and dance.

In addition, many records were reissued in Europe. For example, the main Columbia catalogue for 1932, printed in Zagreb by Columbia Gramophone Jugoslavensko, contains several records by the Hoyer Trio that the group had recorded for Columbia. The stamp on the catalogue makes it clear that it was once the property of Josip Banjaji's Tehnik store at Miklošičeva Street in Ljubljana. The records from the catalogue, including those by the Hoyer Trio, were therefore readily available to Slovenian residents. The catalogue specially emphasizes that this is an "English import" (*Glavni* ... 1932). The selection in the main Columbia catalogue for 1932 indicates that nearly all of the tunes recorded by the Hoyer Trio in the United States were reissued. In this case we can talk about the transnational connections and reciprocal influence on the land of origin. As such the Hoyer Trio did not only help create a Slovenian space in America, with their musical practice and activities they also created a "transnational social space" (cf. Repič 2010: 166).

REFRESH YOUR MEMORIES OF THE DISTANT DAYS OF YOUR YOUTH IN A FAR-OFF HOMELAND

Matt Hoyer spent the first twenty years of his life in the Slovenian countryside. In this period he accumulated cultural capital, which he later benefited from in America. Still in Slovenia he learned how to make and repair accordions, as well as play them (*International* ... s.a.). He must have picked up a lot of melodies in that period, which he would later record on the gramophone records. Among them are a number of tunes which can be defined as folk-dance melodies: *mazulinka*, *pošter tanc*, *treplan – za ples*, *stari šotiš*, *empajris*, *šusterpolka*, *siebernšrit – za ples*, *štajeriš*, and some other polka or waltz melodies. Interestingly, Matt Hoyer made some solo recordings of folk dance melodies, while the trio he played with recorded mostly instrumental music. Singing, accompanied by instrumental music (played by the trio), is rare – predominantly when the recording is done in collaboration with a guest singer or when it involves recordings of well-known Slovenian folk songs. In the latter case the lyrics were sung in the Slovenian language. Slovenian folk dance music from the early 20th century was characteristically "pure" instrumental music. This feature of the dance music was completely lost in the second half of the 20th century, both through its transformation into *narodno-zabavna glasba* (pop-folk music) after World War II in Slovenia as well as with the subsequent development of the musical genre in America. We can count Matt Hoyer among the pioneers of the latter. Singing along with musical accompaniment is typical of the later period of the Cleveland style polka music, which reached its peak with the musical practice of Frank Yankovic (1915–1998), also known as the king of polka. Namely, Frank Yankovic was already translating Slovenian folk songs into English.

Based on listening to the available recordings of the old gramophone records, and partly based only on the titles of the melodies, I classified the recordings of the Hoyer Trio into five categories: polkas, waltzes, marches, folk dances and undefined. Some polkas, waltzes and marches are part of the folk dance repertoire, however they have been excluded from the folk dances category and were included into individual categories, which

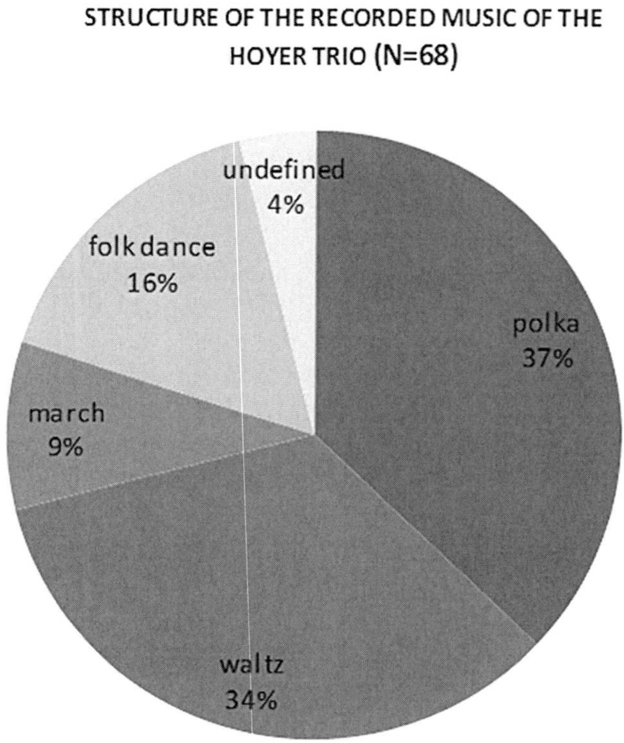

Fig 1: Structure of the recorded music of the Hoyer Trio.

include music of folk origin as well as composed music. Thus the folk dance category includes all the melodies which belong to the remaining folk dances (e.g. *zibenšrit*, *tramplan*, *sotiš*, *mazurka*, *štajeriš*). The results of the analysis of the recorded music structure are presented in the graph (see Figure 1). 16 % of the recorded melodies are in the category of folk dancing, which is not insignificant. Polkas take the biggest share as these are melodies which are enjoyed not only by Slovenians but also by larger audiences/listeners from other European traditions. Thus a decision on what to record partly depended on the individual performer and their preferences and partly on the response and demand of the buyers. These were very likely mostly immigrants who came to America from the rural parts of Europe and by way of recordings wanted to remain connected to their own homeland and culture. These recordings cannot be treated merely as music. They are mainly a tool for bringing back the memories of the hearth at home. Looking at the recordings from today's perspective, these records are music in itself, a real thing, but they can be understood in a slightly different cultural context. Similarly, Thomas Turino (2008: 23–24) says that a music recording can be compared to snapshots of recent vacations the North Americans like to take. In this context music can serve the same purpose as a photograph, as just a tool to remember, it is not the real thing, but a presentation of something else.

For example, the 1925 catalogue *Victorjevi Recordi v Slovenščini* (Victor Records in Slovenian) starts out in Slovenian language by stating: "With the help of Victor, you can hear the music of your native land and enjoy the best and most beautiful sounds of the land where you were born. Refresh your memories of the distant days of your youth in a far-off homeland. The songs that you sang and the music that you danced to is sung and played here by the best and most popular artists, your fellow countrymen" (*Viktorjevi* ... 1925: 1).

COMMERCIAL RECORDINGS (1920') VS. FIELD RESEARCH RECORDINGS (1960')

The majority of the data on folk dance in the Ribnica valley, where Matt Hoyer spent his youth, was collected in the 1960's. Between 1962 and 1966 a systematic collection of folklore material took place, which focused on the folk song. The result of this project were over 600 recorded audio examples, among them several folk dance tunes. Based on the field research from that time a repertoire of folk dances from the area was made (Kumer 1968: 410 –422). I compared this dance repertoire with the dance repertoire made on the basis of the Hoyer Trio discography. The comparison shows that these are very similar selections of folk dances. We can see this in the table below (see Figure 2), which lists the folk dances of the Ribnica valley obtained from the field research. The bold sections represent dances, the instrumental accompaniment of which can also be found on the gramophone records of the Hoyer Trio.

REPERTOIRE OF THE FOLK DANCES FROM THE RIBNICA VALLEY
Abrahama gredo
ajnc – polka
beksl (ples z metlo)
kmečki valček
kolo (pouštr tanc)
koutr šivat
mazulka (mazurka, mazolka)
nojkatoliš
nojpajeriš
pokšotiš (potowčenc, pokčotiš, čotiš, šotiš)
puštrtanc
špicpolka
špigutanc (špeiguček)
štajeriš (oberštajeriš)
šuštarska (šuštar-polka)
tuplirana (potresena polka)
zibenšrit
zic-polka
zmišlaj

Fig. 2: Repertoire of the folk dances from the Ribnica valley.

The table shows that 68 % of the folk-dance repertoire based on the field work had already been recorded by Matt Hoyer 40 years prior to that. As the comparison of material was not entirely based on the audio analysis of the Hoyer Trio recordings, since these were not available to the author, it is likely that this percentage is even higher. It may be that the titles of some recordings which do not imply any correlation to the folk dance hide more tunes from the folk-dance heritage of the Ribnica valley. In addition, some of the recordings contain a medley of folk melodies or combinations of folk melodies and Hoyer's own compositions, as Matt Hoyer was also a composer (Kunej 2008: 194).

The contribution of the old gramophone records is presented in the case of a dance called *zibenšrit*[5], one of the more popular Slovenian folk dances. In her book *Ljudska glasba med rešetarji in lončarji v Ribniški dolini* (Folk music among the sieve makers and potters in the Ribnica Valley; 1968) Zmaga Kumer mentions seven villages from the Ribnica valley where the *zibenšrit* dance was still known in the 1960's. She says: "In some places people can still dance to it, while elswhere they can only remember it" (Kumer 1968: 413). The sound archive of the Institute of Ethnomusicology holds several recordings of the *zibenšrit* melodies from the Ribnica area, which were recorded on tape in the 1960's. One of these was made on 14 March 1965 in Kračali. The *zibenšrit* was played on an accordion by then 73 year old Janez Čampa, who was born in 1892. The recording from Kračali was considered to be one of the oldest audio examples of the *zibenšrit* until we (again) listened to an old gramophone record with Matt Hoyer's recording of *zibenšrit* played on a diatonic accordion. The recording from the record was made in December 1926 in New York, USA, played solo by the 35 year old immigrant from the Ribnica valley, Matt Hoyer, born only a year before Janez Čampa. Their respective birthplaces are only 7 kilometers apart. The "American" recording of *zibenšrit* has been overlooked until now; however, it provides a new piece to the mosaic

5 In the first part the *zibenšrit* has a characteristic structure of seven steps, which are then repeated in the opposite direction. In the second part this is then followed by three steps which are repeated in the opposite direction, which is then followed by a turn. The entire second part is then repeated once again.

of the sonority of Slovenian folk dance music. This recording is also of interest since it was made at the time this dance tradition was still alive. This can be seen from the character and determined way of playing, appropriate tempo—not too fast, as well as a rhythmically suitable performance, as it is easy to dance to the recorded music.

Treating the old gramophone records as an ethnochoreology resource thus provided us with a new example of the *zibenšrit*, which is over thirty years older than the last known oldest recording. However, it was made in the United States. The recordings—the American and the Slovenian, feature two different musicians who were actually born at the same time in the same Slovenian region.

Also other recordings of different folk dance melodies recorded by Matt Hoyer alone or with the Trio have the same musical characteristics of the dance melodies. When I played the available recordings of the Matt Hoyer Trio to some of the experts on Slovenian folk dance they were impressed by the execution and pointed out the suitability of the music for dancing. This is not always the case with the recordings obtained from the field research. Most of the field recordings held in the sound archives of the Institute of Ethnomusicology were collected using the explorative method. As a result the recorded dance tunes are performed in various ways: sung (murmured) or whistled, played by one musician only, just a few dance tunes are recoreded as performances by actual bands with the regular line-up. The researchers have focused their field research on the traditions which were dying out or had completley died out. Consequently, the informants had to recall many dance melodies, although they were not played for their original purpose but only to be recorded by the researcher. It often happened that a musician did not remember the whole dance tune or their psychophysical abilities did not allow for the execution the informants themselves would wish for or that would resemble the way it had been played before. Because of that I believe the question needs to be asked how this dance tune would have sounded if it had been played by the same folk musician 40 years prior, when he was at his peak and the tune was still played for dancing. The commercial recordings on the gramophone records can partially answer this question, even though they come from the other side of the world.

In Kumer's field notes (Kumer 1965: 137) we can read that folk musician Janez Perušek (born 1907) from Podklanec at Ribnica had learned the melodies he played on his accordion from other, older musicians, while others he had learned off gramophone records. Additional information says that he started playing at weddings and other dance events when he was 17 years old, which was in 1924. By that year Perušek's expatriate Matt Hoyer must have made recordings, which were soon available in Slovenia as well. According to newspaper advertisements it was possible to buy some of the records before World War II in several stores in Ljubljana and probably also in other larger Slovenian towns. It was also possible to listen to these records on the radio, although radio itself was a rarity before World War II. Looking at the Radio Ljubljana programme from the 1920's and 1930's we can establish that the Hoyer Trio records were fairly regularly played, usually at least once a week. So such American gramophone records could have at least partially affected the musical practice of Slovenian folk musicians.

CONCLUSION: LOOKING AT ONE THING AND OVERLOOKING THE SAME

The study of the Hoyer Trio records from the perspective of ethnochoreology has brought about new findings and at the same time a new look at the sonority of the folk-dance traditions of Slovenians, even though we are talking about fairly unique types of music—at the same time it is based on Slovenian tradition that is enriched with the popular sonority of America of the time. In addition, the number of folk dance melodies Matt Hoyer and his Trio recorded for the gramophone records show that the dances that Slovenian ethnochoreologists define as folk dances were more present in the 1920's than we often imagine today. I have come to this conclusion by researching old gramophone records, which ethnochoreology research has not yet considered.

There are several reasons for the neglect of old gramophone records as a resource in the research of folk dance. First, there is the attitude of ethnochoreology to the dance and the accompanying music, which primarily is focused on the research of the array of dance forms and their variations. The accompanying dance music served "only" as the background and was thus secondary to the research of ethnochoreologists. The research of folk dance music has remained the subject of ethnomusicologists, who have rarely dealt with that topic due to the vastness of their original field of interest.

The reason why gramophone records have been overlooked is partly due to the fact that gramophone record production is associated with mass and popular culture, even though the old gramophone records are a form of audio carriers, which have preserved some of the Slovenian musical heritage from the first half of the 20th century. It seems that the records were considered to be incompatible with the study of folk music and dance, both of which are supposed to operate under different principles of life and preservation than other music genres. In reality there is only one music, which coexists in space and time in different forms—this includes popular as well as folk forms.

The criteria of what is "worth" researching in the field of folk dance differs from one individual researcher to another according to their preferences and ideologies. Field research has always been of primary importance together with the need to document everything which would eventually be forgotten (with the death of the informants). Finally, we can perceive the old gramophone records as audio recordings of the immaterial. It is often believed that significant work has been done by documenting and transforming the immaterial into the material form and further research on this topic could wait for a while.

Since World War II technology has played an important role in the fact that gramophone records have not been considered as a resource for ethnochoreology research. Special equipment is needed in order to play 78 rpm records. With the technical development of new audio carriers and the corresponding audio players this equipment was becoming less and less accessible after World War II. The audio material on the old gramophone records has again become available to researchers only with the development of the digitalisation process in the last two decades, which gives researchers a way to listen to the recorded content once again.

There is no institution in Slovenia that purposely collects and creates collections of old gramophone records, which is the primary reason for the complete lack of use of this material in the ethnochoreological and ethnomusicological research in Slovenia. Individual old gramophone records thus appear in various collections of different institutions, for example in the Music Collection of the National and University Library, the audio archives of the Institute of Ethnomusicology, the Technical Museum of Slovenia, the Slovene Ethnographic Museum, while copies can also be found in the Radio Slovenia archives. In Slovenia, unlike other countries, there are no collectors of old gramophone records. Individual collectors own only several records besides old gramophone players. As for the Hoyer Trio records, probably the biggest collection of their gramophone records can be found in The National Cleveland-Style Polka Hall of Fame in Euclid, Cleveland, USA. Most likely a number of records can also be found in private collections abroad.

To conclude, material recorded on 78 rpm phonograph discs has exceptional ethnochoreological value because most of them represent the oldest sound recordings of Slovenian instrumental folk dance music. The oldest field recordings of Slovenian instrumental folk dance music were made much later, after 1955, when the Institute of Ethnomusicology in Ljubljana acquired its first tape recorder and started making systematic field recordings.

In order to control the subject of interest researchers have divided the definition of folklore into genres, categories and other definitions and breakdowns. This is to help us define different performance practices, their features of style and products. However, we forget that the boundaries of folklore as well as our definitions can be very fluid and difficult to define, changeable and inconclusive. By cementing these boundaries we can become trapped in folklore, always looking only at the folk music and folk dance, but forgetting to look over the picket fence to the neighbour called popular, mass or commercial music. And thus, because of our fixation with one, we overlook the same in the other.

REFERENCES

Glavni ...
1932 *Glavni katalog Columbia 1932. Engleski import. Samo električne snimke.* Zagreb: Columbia Graphophone Jugoslavensko d. d.

International ...
s.a. *International Polka Association. Matt Hoyer.* http://www.internationalpolka.com/hoyer.htm (accessed 22 Avgust 2011).

Kumer, Zmaga
1965 Podklanec, 28. 1. 1965 (field notes). In: *Terenski zvezek 16. Ribniška dolina 1963–1966.* Ljubljana: Arhiv, Glasbenonarodopisni inštitut ZRC SAZU, 137–141.
1968 *Ljudska glasba med rešetarji in lončarji v Ribniški dolini.* Maribor: Založba obzorja.

Kunej, Drago
1999 Prva magnetofonska snemanja zvočnega gradiva Glasbenonarodopisnega inštituta. *Traditiones* 28 (2): 217–232.
2008 *Fonograf je dospel! Prvi zvočni zapisi slovenske ljudske glasbe.* Ljubljana: Založba ZRC.
2012 Slovenian recordings made by the Favorite company in Ljubljana in 1910. In: Gronow, Pekka, and Christiane Hofer (eds.), *The Lindström Project: Contributions to the history of the record industry.* Vol. 4. Wien: Gesellschaft für Historische Tonträger, 44–50.

Ramovš, Mirko
1992 *Polka je ukazana. Plesno izročilo na Slovenskem: Gorenjska, Dolenjska, Notranjska.* Ljubljana: Kres.
2005 Plesna dediščina. In: Prešeren, Damjana, and Nataša Gorenc (eds.), *Nesnovna kulturna dediščina.* Ljubljana: Zavod za varstvo kulturne dediščine Slovenije, 89–102.

Repič, Jaka
2010 Konstrukcija prostora in kraja pri transnacionalnih migracijah med Argentino in Slovenijo. In: Mencej, Mirjam, and Dan Podjed

(eds.), *Ustvarjanje prostorov.* Ljubljana: Znanstvena založba Filozofske fakultete, 162–188.

Terselic, Richard A., and Charles F. Debevec
2009 Preserving Old American-Slovenian Recorded Music. *Slovene Studies. Journal of the society for Slovene Studies* 31 (2): 195–200.

The National ...
s.a. *The National Cleveland-Style Polka Hall of Fame. Hoyer, Matt.* http://www.clevelandstyle.com/awards_lifetime_Hoyer_Matt.html (accessed 22 Avgust 2011).

Turino, Thomas
2008 *Music as Social Life. The Politics of Participation.* Chicago and London: The University of Chicago Press.

Victorjevi ...
1925 *Victorjevi Recordi v Slovenščini. Victor records in Slovenian.* New Jersey: Victor Talking Machine Company.

Vprašanje ...
1933 Vprašanje slovenskih plošč. *Radio Ljubljana. Ilustrirani tednik za radiofonijo* 5 (17): 193.

Drago Kunej

DIGITISED EARLY SOUND RECORDINGS AS SCHOLARLY RESOURCES

ABSTRACT

The article discusses the advantages and disadvantages of audio material with a focus on digitised early sound recordings and gives basic directions for the critical use and interpretation of historical sound documents as a good audio resource for users and researchers in various disciplines. Although recordings contain much more information than a precise transcription or notation, sound recordings also have to be understood as only one of the possible ways to record a performance and one should also bear in mind their incompleteness.

Key words: historical sound recordings, mechanical sound carriers, rotational speed, playback, digitised folk music

INTRODUCTION

Studying music using sound recordings offers several advantages compared to studying it from transcriptions. Specifically, sound recordings allow one to perceive music in the most basic way: listening. The considerable limitations and incompleteness of musical notation offer only a basic and incomplete representation of music and sound because the essence of sound is missing: the actual sound itself with all the details of its interpretation, dynamics, tempo, timbre, and so on. Therefore, ethnomusicology and folklore studies often consider sound recordings an almost perfect scholarly resource for studying folk music, even though this belief is fairly naive and lacks any real theoretical bases (cf. Schüller 1992, Schüller 1994). Researchers are thus too frequently trapped in an insufficiently critical mode of using various sound recordings and tend to trust them too blindly as reliable scholarly resources when conducting research in ethnomusicology and folklore studies.

However, a sound recording is not a complete scholarly resource because the perception and understanding of music is affected by many technical and methodological recording factors, as well as acoustic, psychological, and sociological factors when playing back the recorded material. Although recordings contain much more information than a precise transcription or notation, sound recordings also have to be understood as only one of the possible ways to record a performance and one should also bear in mind their incompleteness.

This is especially true for recordings in ethnomusicology, particularly for early sound recordings. Because of the limited technical abilities of the first recording devices and today's lack of technology and expertise for playing back and interpreting early sound recordings, these can represent a deficient and even a misleading scholarly resource. For early sound recordings, which are largely available in the form of copied recordings, it is also important to be aware of the technical parameters and the process of playing back, re-recording, and digitising the original sound medium because this has a decisive impact on what is heard on the recording.

The optimal digitising of historical sound recordings is not easy. Before digitising a recording, it is of paramount importance to understand the historical recording, the carrier and the recording circumstances and to collect information and documentation about the technology used, the performance method, the performers, and so on. As presented further into the paper it is crucial to know technical, methodological and other parameters which influence the recorded signal.

Based on an analysis of some of the most important changes that develop while listening to a sound recording even just by changing the playback speed (rotational speed), this article answers what needs to be provided in order for the digitised sound recordings to serve as a good scholarly resource.

UNDERSTANDING EARLY ETHNOMUSICOLOGY FIELD RECORDINGS

Throughout the entire early period of ethnomusicology field recordings, the recording process was quite similar to the first studio recordings with the phonograph. The only difference was that field researchers generally did not have as much equipment as recording operators in studios, nor was their equipment as advanced. They were often unfamiliar with the recording process and how to handle the phonograph, and they usually recorded various ensembles with performers that were not accustomed to being recorded. Folk music was not well-suited to the awkward conditions of early sound recording. Therefore field phonograph recordings, even taking into account the technical capabilities of the phonograph, do not attain the quality that might be expected and was desired, and that studio recordings of that time did achieve. Moreover, each field recording generally represented the only one of its kind.

From today's perspective, the very narrow frequency range of the recordings is particularly bothersome; in the best of circumstances, this was between 100 and 5,000 Hz for cylinders (Fadeyev et al. 2003), and in field recordings made with smaller and simpler phonographs it was somewhere between 300 and 3,500 Hz. The recorded sound is therefore considerably impaired and acoustically colored. In song recordings the lyrics are often difficult to understand, and in instrumental recordings it is difficult to recognise the instruments. In addition, the recordings are often distorted because the recording horn and membrane introduced considerable nonlinearity into the recording, combined with the relatively poor manner and execution of the recording. This was exacerbated by the drive mechanism of the phonograph, which did not run completely smoothly and also created low-frequency noise, which is audible in the recording due to the mechanical transmission of sound. The manner of recording itself did not allow dynamics in the performance because for a good recording it was necessary to have a fairly strong and uniform sound source. Because of the poor sensitivity of the phonograph, on the recordings it is not possible to hear reverberation, or the acoustics of the room, which creates a rather isolated, empty, and unnatural sound during playback.

It is also necessary to emphasise the fact that mechanical carriers are gradually worn down each time they are played; this was especially evident when they were played back on the original devices with acoustic pickups, which pressed relatively heavily into the groove. Because of the softer construction necessary for recording sound, the wax cylinders used for field recording were even more sensitive to abrasion during playback than were cast cylinders and pressed discs.

Technical imperfections (e.g. the rather poor sensitivity of the device and the limitation of the length of cylinder recordings to two to four minutes) often led to methodological drawbacks in field recording. As a result, the performers had to be very close to the horn and stand as still as possible during recording. In addition, the performance had to be relatively loud and clear. This was likely to create a certain amount of tension among the performers due to the unnatural conditions, which had an effect on the performance itself and the resulting recording (cf. Kunej 2008).

PLAYING BACK EARLY SOUND CARRIERS

The first, and most significant, part of the digitisation process is optimising signal retrieval from the original carriers (Bradley 2009: 31), a fact that is often overlooked. When playing back historical carriers as scholarly resources, the aim is to reproduce as much recorded information in its original form as possible. The criteria to be taken into account are purely academic and not esthetic. Such playback is not trivial because, apart from the appropriate equipment, much specialised knowledge about playing back historical carriers is needed. Moreover, the carrier, which is often in very poor and fragile condition, must not be damaged further or even destroyed during the process.

The first thing that needs to be established is the technical parameters required for playing back and then setting up the playback equipment accordingly. The basic playback parameters include the playback speed (rotational speed) of the carrier, the playback needle and pick up, the equalisation curve and filtering, and preparation of the carrier for the playback procedure. These parameters can be the determining factors in the sound signal obtained and are therefore crucial for maintaining its credibility as a resource for ethnomusicological research. It is often not simple to set the parameters correctly because early ethnomusicological recordings are frequently not accompanied by extensive documentation, especially as far as the technical aspect of the recordings is concerned. This is why the recording and technical settings are often established from other resources and knowledge about the technology of that time. If the parameters are chosen frivolously and subjectively, or if one relies on contemporary musical esthetics and taste, the resulting reproductions could be far from true to the original.

CARRIER PLAYBACK SPEED (ROTATIONAL SPEED)

One of the most important parameters in playing back mechanical sound carriers is the carrier rotational speed. This has a direct impact on various other aspects that influence the sound and the sound recording: tempo of music and speech, intonation of the recording, sound color of the recording, performer's style (e.g. musical ornaments, the dramatic impact of speech), and so on. The playback speed of the carrier also influences the subjective perception of the recorded material, such as the intelligibility of the recorded speech and text, the natural sound of instruments and voices, and the esthetic impression of the recorded music and speech.

Recordings that are intended to serve as scholarly resources must be played back independent of listeners' wishes and tastes and must follow the original performance. This is why early sound archives that used field recordings for research purposes documented the recording speed in detail (e.g. the Vienna Phonogrammarchiv) or they included a reference tone such as a^1 concert pitch in the recording (e.g. the Berlin Phonogramm-Archiv), which was used in all the subsequent playback sessions to determine the appropriate recording speed. This is important because the only way to ensure the original sound effect is for mechanical sound carriers to be played back at the same speed as the one used when the recording was made (cf. Bradley 2009: 39). Unfortunately, many of the early sound recordings were made without following any standards and providing any accompanying technical documentation, which is why the recording sound carrier rotational speed is not known in these cases. The rotational speed of field phonographs was set by winding a special screw or moving a handle, and a considerable range could be selected. Cylinders were commonly recorded at a speed anywhere from 80 up to 250 revolutions per minute (cf. Wiedmann 2000: 208).

Fig. 1: Part of a field phonograph with the handle for selection of the rotational speed; in this model speeds from 100 rpm to 160 rpm could be selected. Foto: Drago Kunej, 2006.

Old gramophone records pose special difficulties in determining the correct rotational speed. These were supposed to have been recorded at a rotational speed of 78 rpm, which is why they are often referred to as 78s. However, the rotational speed of 78 rpm was only standardised after 1930.

Before that time, recording rotational speeds generally ranged between 70 and 85 rpm, but speeds anywhere from 60 to 130 rpm were possible (*Technical* ... s.a.: 1). In various time periods, record companies used different "official" rotational speeds for their recording, most of which they tended not to document or indicate; moreover, when they did so, these were often inaccurate (cf. Wilmut s.a., Copeland 2008). It is also interesting that, due to different frequencies in the power grid (60 Hz in the U.S. and 50 Hz in Europe) during the electrical recording period (i.e. after 1925), the rotational speeds of records during recording were not the same in the U.S. and Europe. The difference between these two speeds is relatively small and difficult to perceive, but some people can hear it if they listen carefully. Several attempts have already been made to try to establish the recording rotational speeds for specific time periods of some major record producers, but this has not proved successful. It turned out that the rotation frequencies also differed between the recording devices, individual recording studios, and recording egineers (cf. Moran 1986: 7).

Thus it is to be expected that both acoustic and electrical recordings made before 1930 are likely to sound "off-key" when played back—perhaps even a whole tone or more—if the rotational speed has not been carefully determined. Therefore, in order to conduct an accurate analysis of the material recorded on gramophone records one needs to determine the appropriate playback speed, especially in the case of early recordings, using various methods and in a similar way as with wax cylinder recordings.

In determining the suitable playback speed various data accompanying the recordings (metadata) can be of great help; these include documented recording rotational speed, recorded reference tones, and other sources connected with the recorded material such as potential musical notation of the recorded material, already existing transcriptions, and so on. In addition, various methods for assessing the suitable playback speed such as the method based on the feel and timbre of known sounds on the recording can also be helpful. All of these sources and methods have their strengths and weaknesses, and are to a certain extent unreliable, and so for best precision it is recommended that multiple methods and sources be used together.

Without the detailed accompanying technical documentation it is therefore very difficult to determine what the appropriate rotational speed for recordings on mechanical carriers might be. Three methods are briefly presented below that are commonly used to determine the playback speed for mechanical carriers.

Method based on documented recording rotational speed

This is the simplest method, but it is also not always the most reliable. It is based on the documented rotational speed when the mechanical carrier is recorded, indicated by the number of rotations per minute. The number of phonograph rotations was defined by counting the turns of the cylinder per time unit; in practice, the number of rotations was counted for a quarter or half minute, and the result was multiplied accordingly. The reliability of speed determined in this way primarily depends on the skill of the person that counts the revolutions, and partially on the rotational speed as well because at high speeds it is difficult to reliably count the turns. An additional source of error was the shortened counting period because multiplying the number of revolutions could multiply any error as well. Experience and measurements have shown that this method is relatively useful for speeds up to about 150 rpm; after this, counting errors increase considerably and the rotational speed information can become unreliable (cf. Kunej 2006: 183). This error can even surpass 12 % at the playback speeds about 190 rpm, which creates a change in intonation of more than 200 cents, or more than one whole tone.

Method based on recorded reference tones

Defining the playback speed by using a recorded reference tone is a very reliable and relatively simple method. This means of documentation was already used by some very early folk music researchers because the reference tone later aided them greatly during transcription (cf. Dovhalyuk 1999). The Berlin Phonogramm-Archiv also extensively used this documentation method because in their study of "exotic" music cultures they largely depended on correct interpretation of the recorded material. Point D of the audio recording section in the fifth edition of the instructions for ethnographic research and collection published in 1908 says the following: "Every recording begins such that the tone *a* is played into the device with a whistle" (*Anleitung* ... 1908: 1). Later on, it was established that recording a reference tone at the beginning of a recording automatically affected the performers, the majority of whom followed this intonation in their performace. Therefore, the reference tone began to be recorded at the end of the recording. Then it happened that the desire to obtain as long a recording of the performers as possible meant there was often no room left for the reference tone in the end.

It is necessary to emphasise that the frequency of concert pitch a^1 once varied considerably, from as low as 375 to as high as 567 Hz. In 1859 it was standardised at 435 Hz, in 1939 recommended to change to 440 Hz and in 1953 standardised at 440 Hz (Ravnikar 1999: 41). However, even during the time of standardised values these were not always consistently used. To precisely define the playback speed it is therefore necessary to know the precise value of the reference tone on the recording.

The reliability of this method primarily depends on the precision of the recorded reference tone and the ability to define its pitch because, as a rule, the playback speed is defined by listening to the pitch of the reference tone. Based on experience, it can be concluded that by listening to the reference tone a skilled listener can precisely define the appropriate playback speed, which almost never deviates from the frequency measure of the reference tone.

Method based on feel and timbre of known sounds on the recording

In the absence of more objective information about the recording speed, a common method is to define the playback speed based on the feel and timbre of known sounds on the recording. This method is very simple but it can also be quite unreliable, especially if the recorded material is unfamiliar. The very narrow frequency range of old recordings also represents a great difficulty. This impedes the understandability of the content because in extreme cases it is not possible to clearly recognise the sound source (e.g. the instrument on the recording) or to distinguish it from other instruments and sounds, let alone to determine its natural sound.

The reliability of this method primarily depends on our ability to define an appropriate timbre for a recognised sound or its natural color on the recording. Some have concluded from experience that it is easier to determine errors at the lower limit of playback speed (a recording that is too slow) than at the higher limit (a recording that is too fast), and they therefore suggest that one should first define the lower limit of acceptable sound and then raise it somewhat (Wilmut s.a.). My own experience indicates that in general it is easier to judge the appropriate playback speed for speech than for singing.

It turns out that defining the appropriate speed based on impressions while listening is not as reliable as might be expected and as phonograph producers stated. For example, one set of instructions for using the phonograph states that the playback speed can be set as one wishes by tightening and loosening a special screw, which primarily influences the pitch of the sound, and that "setting the speed is very simple and even the unskilled ear can find the right setting on the first attempt" (*Instructions* ... s.a.). This optimistic assertion by the producers does not hold at all for field recordings of folk music, and often not for other types of recordings either.

This is also shown by a listening test that was conducted at the ZRC SAZU Institute of Ethnomusicology. Participants listened to part of a song that we copied at five playback speeds (147 rpm, 175 rpm, 185 rpm, 196 rpm, and 208 rpm), which created a corresponding change in each copy (intonation, tempo, timbre etc.). Based on what they heard, the listeners then judged which playback version of the singing seemed the most natural or correct, and which the least. Their responses are presented in Figure 2.

The bar graph indicates that clearly the least appropriate playback speed seemed to be 208 rpm, and in some cases also 147 rpm. However, for some participants 147 rpm was also most appropriate. Most participants chose 175 rpm as the most appropriate speed, followed by 185 rpm, and fewer chose 196 rpm as the most appropriate.

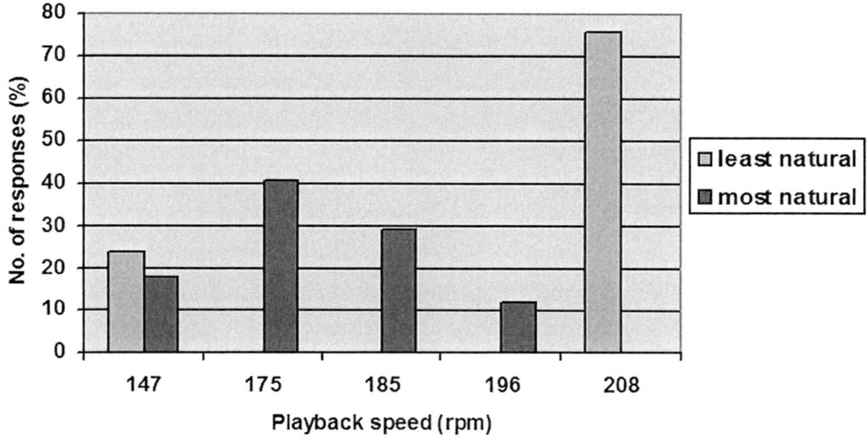

Fig. 2: Responses on the naturalness of singing on wax cylinder recordings when played back at various speeds.

This example shows that defining the appropriate playback speed of mechanical carriers based on the subjective feel of a sound can be rather unreliable. It also depends on the quality of the recording and on the type of audio material. Familiarity with the performers, their manner of singing and playing, and characteristics of the instruments used can often be of help in judging the appropriate speed. However, it is also necessary to exercise caution because folk musicians, for example, often tune their instruments more "freely" or differently compared to what we are accustomed to today.

THE INFLUENCE OF PLAYBACK SPEED ON PERCEIVING AND UNDERSTANDING A RECORDING

The purpose of the listening test was also to evaluate how different copies of recordings influence the perception and interpretation of material on recordings, such as recognition of the lyrics and the sex, number, and age of singers, as well as the quality of the recorded material, such as the sound of instruments, the quality of the performers and their performance, and the technical quality of the recording. Information on recognising the singers' sex is cited as an example.

It is primarily the speed of playing back sound carriers that affects the perception of the singers' sex. Although certain major changes in playback speed create a perceptibly unnatural sound in the recording and such playback can be rejected as inappropriate, certain changes in speed are such that they can be perceived as a change in the singers' sex. In order to determine the impression of the singers' sex, our survey included several different questions and sound recordings, and participants were asked about the sex of the singers on various recordings. The first set of the recordings was copied at a speed of 147 rpm, and the second set at 185 rpm. Analysis of the participants' responses and our own experience in listening to the copies

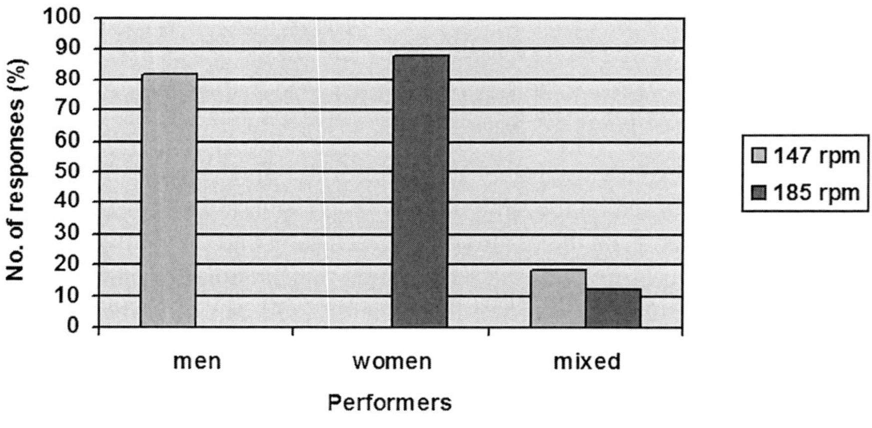

Fig. 3: Responses on the sex of singers when listening to the same song copied at 147 rpm and 185 rpm.

indicate that various playback speeds can completely change the impression of the singers' sex. Copies made at 147 rpm overwhelmingly give the impression of male singers, even though the singers were actually mixed or even only female. In contrast, listening to copies made at 185 rpm overwhelmingly gives the impression of mixed groups or female singers, which is closer to the actual state of affairs that can be understood from the accompanying metadata. One example of such findings is presented in Figure 3.

CONCLUSION

Because of the change in playback speed, the recordings were experienced in a completely new light by the listeners. In the example described above we changed the playback speed by about 26 %, which caused a corresponding change in the tempo of the performance and raised the intonation by about two tones or 400 cents. The change in the impression of the performers and singing was even more significant. Instead of the impression of male (or predominantly male) singers, there was an impression of female singers or a mixed group. In addition, the manner of performance was different because certain performance characteristics (e.g. the tempo of singing, the intonation of individual sounds, musical ornamentation etc.) were presented quite differently. For ethnomusicology researchers, such copies of cylinder recordings are becoming a completely different scholarly resource.

Therefore it is very important that copies of old audio recordings be evaluated and assessed as resources before they are used for scholarly purposes. This is especially important when there is no access to the original recordings and carriers or when these carriers have already been damaged or destroyed, and thus the copies are the only available source of the audio material. In the modern era of digital audio formats it is also important that one knows how to evaluate the copy based on the sound signal because in the digital format many data that originated from the mechanical carrier (e.g. the type and condition of the carrier, any written comments on it or the box or cover etc.) can no longer be retrieved. In addition to a good knowledge of the historical, technical, methodological, and other conditions at the time when the recordings and their copies were being made, certain acoustic-technical analysies of the copies can also be of great help. Through various measurements and analyses of time and frequency signals on the copy and by comparing it to other copies, one can determine certain settings and parameters that were used during digitisation and can thus evaluate the copy better, determine the effect of the digitising technology on the audio material, and thus influence the interpretation of the recorded material. Based on our analyses it can be concluded that the technical quality of the reproduction not only influences the aesthetic perception of the recording but that it also has an impact on the perception and evaluation of the recorded content and performers, a fact that must be borne in mind in ethnomusicological research.

From the scholarly and archival points of view, it is very important to play back and digitise recordings with the best possible equipment that is adapted to playing back old recordings, and in doing so to utilise the greatest possible knowledge, experience, and accompanying information, because this is the only way to suitably play back and make copies of old audio material, interpret it appropriately, and use it for scholarly study. Furthermore, it is of paramount importance that all the accompanying documentation and other resources containing information about the recordings are collected before making the digitisation, that no interventions are made in the signal during reproduction, and that the reproduction process is thoroughly documented with all the equipment that has been used and its reproduction parameters. Old sound recordings, which are critically influenced by certain methodological and technical parameters of recording and later playback, are defined by these parameters. Accompanying information (i.e. metadata) about the performers, the performance method, the recording circumstances, the technology used, the historical circumstances, and so on can greatly contribute to defining certain technical parameters during playback and digitising recordings from old carriers, and all of this together contributes to evaluating recordings as scholarly resources. Only such digital archive copies with metadata serve as the best possible resource for current and future ethnomusicological and other research.

REFERENCES

Anleitung ...
1908 *Anleitung für ethnographische Beobachtungen und Sammlungen in Afrika und Oceanien.* Fünfte Auflage. Berlin: Königliches Museum für Völkerkunde in Berlin.

Bradley, Kevin (ed.)
2009 *Guidelines on the production and preservation of digital audio objects (IASA Technical Committee – Standards, Recommended Practices and Strategies, IASA-TC 04)*, second edition. Canberra: International Association of Sound and Audiovisual Archives (IASA).

Copeland, Peter
2008 *Manual of Analogue Sound Restoration Techniques.* London: The British Library. http://www.bl.uk/reshelp/findhelprestype/sound/anaudio/analoguesoundrestoration.pdf (accessed 20 August 2010).

Dovgaljuk, Iryna (Dovhal'uk, Iryna)
1999 Fonoarhiv Osypa Rozdol'skogo. *Visnyk L'vivs'kogo Universytetu, Serija filologična,* vyp. 27: 164–170.

Fadeyev, Vitaliy et al.
2003 Reconstruction of Mechanically Recorded Sound from an Edison Cylinder using Three Dimensional Non-Contact Optical Surface Metrology. http://www-cdf.lbl.gov/~av/cylinder-paper-PVF.pdf (accessed 22 September 2005).

Instructions ...
1903 *Instructions pour se servir du phonographe "XXc siècle". Dernière création – modèle 1903.* http://www.archeophone.org/catalogues (accessed 6 September 2004).

Kunej, Drago
2006 *Optimalno predvajanje, restavriranje in uporaba prvih slovenskih etnomuzikoloških zvočnih zapisov* (doctoral dissertation). Ljubljana: Univerza v Ljubljani, Akademija za glasbo.

2008 *Fonograf je dospel! Prvi zvočni zapisi slovenske ljudske glasbe.* Ljubljana: Založba ZRC.

Moran, Bill
1986 Disc Playback Speed. *Encyclopedic Discography of Victor Recordings.* http://victor.library.ucsb.edu/index.php/resources/detail/58 (accessed 20 August 2010).

Ravnikar, Bruno
1999 *Osnove glasbene akustike in informatike.* Ljubljana: Državna Založba Slovenije.

Schüller, Dietrich
1992 Phonographische Dokumentationsmethoden in der Ethnomusicologie. In: Lipp, Wolfgang (ed.), *Gesselschaft und Musik. Wege zur Musiksoziologie.* Berlin: Dunker & Humblot, 505–517.

1994 Mikrophonverfahren für ethnomuzikologische Schallaufnahmen. In: Hilscher, Elisabeth Th., and Theophil Antonicek (eds.), *Vergleichend-systematische Musikwissenschaft. Beiträge zur Methode und Problematik der systematischen, ethnologischen und historischen Musikforschung. Franz Födermayr zum 60. Geburtstag.* Tutzing: Hans Schneider, 119–144.

Technical ...
s.a. Technical Issues & Options. http://www.78.com/rescat/tech_info_page.htm (accessed 22 May 2005).

Wiedmann, Albrecht
2000 A few Technical Remarks on the Digital Conservation of the Old Inventory of the Berlin Phonogramm-Archiv. In: Simon, Artur (ed.), *The Berlin Phonogramm-Archiv 1900–2000. Collections of Traditional Music of the World.* Berlin: VWB – Verlag für Wiessenschaft und Bildung, 203–208.

Wilmut, Roger
s.a. Reproduction of 78rpm records. http://www.rfwilmut.clara.net/repro78/repro.html (accessed 22 July 2005).

Susanne Ziegler

WHAT TO DO WITH HISTORICAL RECORDINGS? EXPERIENCES FROM THE BERLIN PHONOGRAMM-ARCHIV

ABSTRACT

Historical recordings form a valuable basis for the research of music worldwide, but they are often trapped in archives and not open to public access. This paper focuses on the historical wax cylinder collections preserved in the Berlin Phonogramm-Archiv. The collections cover a time span from 1893 until 1954 and specialise in traditional music from all over the world including folklore. The author provides insight into archiving, preservation, and digitisation strategies and discusses different possibilities of access.

Key words: historical recordings, wax cylinders, Phonogramm-Archiv, access, preservation strategies

INTRODUCTION

Historical recordings form a valuable basis for research on music worldwide. But what do we understand by the term "historical recordings?" Are these recordings connected with a special time, or does the term refer to the audio format that enables us to speak about "historical recordings?"

In common archival understanding, the term "historical recordings" is a combination of both, because special sound carriers and the respective machines were used only within a limited time span. In general, sound recordings to be used for scientific research should have the best quality, and not all machines on the market fulfil this precondition. Specifically, for ethnomusicological documentation and research phonographs, wax cylinders and wax plates were in use from 1900 until the early 1950s; recordings on tape started in the late 1930s and were used up to the 1970s. From the 1970s onwards recordings on analogue cassettes were made, but they are not regarded as substantial, durable archival sources. Digital cassettes (R-DAT) have been widely used in ethnomusicological field work, but new equipment is now virtually unavailable. Today recording on hard disc is the most common device.

The need for establishing sound archives arose at the end of the 19th/beginning of the 20th century, and most of the archives have continued until the present day; hence, they have to deal with different kinds of historical sources.[1] Some of these archives were founded in order to focus on the national musical idiom, as in Croatia, Romania, Sweden etc., while others went beyond national borders and specialised on traditional music from all over the world. Besides the Vienna Phonogrammarchiv, founded in 1899, the Berlin Phonogramm-Archiv is among the most famous archives in the world. Both archives are "researched-based audiovisual archives" (Seeger 2010: 14). Whereas the Vienna Phonogrammarchiv is well-known and used by the international scientific community, the Berlin Phonogramm-Archiv is less known, which is due to its post-war history, but also to the different composition of the holdings.[2]

The holdings in the Berlin Phonogramm-Archiv comprise thousands of historical recordings on wax cylinders (Ziegler 2006). The problems that arise when dealing with wax cylinders are manifold: The technical quality of the wax cylinder recordings is generally rather poor, and, in addition, because of repeated playing many cylinders were worn out before they were galvanised.[3] On the other hand, the content of the recordings is in many cases extraordinarily valuable, since no other recordings from that time, region or musical genre exist. Compared to later recordings and also to commercial recordings on discs, these early cylinder recordings present unique material; in general they represent the earliest recordings, which are

1 For more information on handling different kinds of historical sound carriers see Bradley 2009.

2 An overview on 100 years of ethnomusicological recording can be found in Simon and Wegner 2000.

3 For a detailed description of wax cylinder techniques applied in the Berlin Phonogramm-Archiv cf. Wiedmann 2006: 35.

of the greatest importance for ethnomusicology and folk music research worldwide. This has also been acknowledged by the inscription of the "Early wax cylinder recordings of the Berlin Phonogramm-Archiv" in the UNESCO-list "Memory of the World" in 1999; it is further confirmed by the many requests and visitors from all over the world asking for historical recordings. However, when it comes to the sound quality, these recordings do not fulfil the high expectations of the listener/researcher.

There is an ongoing discussion about safeguarding the audio heritage of the world[4]; however, problems connected with wax cylinders have not been discussed at length, since this audio format is represented in only a few sound archives. The large collection of wax cylinders in the Berlin Phonogramm-Archiv has a long-lasting history; many cylinders suffered under poor storage conditions, evacuation, several moves and therefore different kinds of problems have arisen. The archive's task is to decide what to do with the wax cylinder recordings. Should they be preserved in the original state, should they be restored in a time and money consuming process, or could they also be thrown away if damaged? Furthermore, following A. Seeger (2010: 16), one could also ask, whether the result is worth the effort.

This article provides insight into the Phonogramm-Archiv's efforts in archiving, preserving, and providing access to the historical wax cylinder recordings. The cylinders in Berlin are a special challenge because of their history and their great value for ethnomusicology. My intention is to show how the Archive deals with the wax cylinder collections by considering the different tasks that sound archives have according to IASA Technical Committee publication (Schüller 2005). In order not to have the cylinder collections trapped in the Archive out of access and use, various efforts are being made to preserve, digitise and thus render the recorded material available to the public.

4 For example Schüller 2005, Bradley 2009, Gütl et al. 2010, Seeger and Chaudhuri 2004 to cite just a few.

THE BERLIN PHONOGRAMM-ARCHIV AT PRESENT

The Berlin Phonogramm-Archiv, today part of the Ethnomusicology Department of the Ethnological Museum in Berlin (formerly the Museum für Völkerkunde), comprises one of the finest and most comprehensive collections of traditional music worldwide. Throughout its history of more than one hundred years, the Berlin Phonogramm-Archiv has devoted its activities to the collection of traditional music and its research from the various cultures of the world. While the sound carriers and recording techniques have changed, the purpose of the sound archive has remained the same: the

Fig. 1: Edison Home Phonograph and wax cylinders from the collections of the Berlin Phonogramm-Archiv. Ethnologisches Museum, Staatliche Museen zu Berlin – Preußischer Kulturbesitz, 2002. Photo: Martin Franken.

collection, preservation, research and publication of the world's musical traditions.[5]

The historical collections preserved in the Berlin Phonogramm-Archiv encompass more than 30,000 cylinders (original cylinders, matrices and copies) from almost all areas of the world, which were recorded with a phonograph between 1893 and 1954.

Within the 351 collections, comprising between one or more than one thousand cylinders, the greatest part stems from the former German colonies in Africa and the South Pacific. The recordings range from non-Western music in a variety of songs of traditional as well as of popular, secular and ritual character, musical instruments, examples of foreign languages and speech, experimental recordings and a few examples of Western music.

In addition to the sound examples, written material such as documentation about the recorded music (the so-called "Journale"), the correspondence between the collector and the Berlin Phonogramm-Archiv, publications related to the respective collection, transcriptions, and in most cases also photos and ethnographical objects (musical instruments) have been collected as well and are available to the researcher.[6] The wax cylinder collections in the Berlin Phonogramm-Archiv form the foundation stone for the university subject "ethnomusicology" or—in the beginning—"comparative musicology," and this is the reason why they are extraordinary significant and valuable for the history of our discipline.

WAX CYLINDERS AND ARCHIVAL RESPONSIBILITIES

Wax cylinders form a special kind of historical sound carriers: on the one hand, a cylinder is a fragile object which has to be preserved as an object itself, on the other hand, the important information is not the cylinder, but the information it carries. The hidden information is not available at first

5 See also Simon 2000.

6 For more information on the history and holdings of the Berlin Phonogramm-Archiv see Ziegler 2006.

glance, but has to be made audible with the help of machines like the phonograph. During the recording session the object, the wax cylinder, has been connected to the invisible sound, and for the future these two elements are irrevocably connected. The sound can be transferred to another sound carrier; yet when separated from the wax cylinder, the sound looses its history. On the other hand: wax cylinders are objects, but it is not easy to determine whether they carry sound and specifically, what kind of sound.

In addition, the majority of the cylinder collection in Berlin does not represent original wax cylinders, but copper negatives that are treated as originals. These so called "galvanos" were produced from the original cylinders in order to prevent the loss of sound quality by repeated playback and to provide copies upon request.[7]

In the Berlin Phonogramm-Archiv the cylinders are treated not only as sound carriers, but also as ethnographical objects, which are closely linked with ethnological or archaeological expeditions. In this context they are also made available for exhibitions and loan, one of the Berlin Phonogramm-Archiv's distinctions from other sound archives.[8] Therefore the responsibility is twofold: As far as the object itself is concerned, the responsibility lies within the restoration department, and there is no doubt that the cylinders (original wax cylinders, galvano-matrices, and copies) should be preserved and handled properly like other ethnographical objects in the museum. The sound archive's responsibility, on the other hand, is to make the content of the cylinder available, to identify the recording, and to preserve the sound on digital sound carriers according to the IASA guidelines (Bradley 2009: 32). It is also the intention of the archive to keep up with ongoing research in the field of endangered sound carriers.[9]

7 Cf. Hornbostel 1923.

8 Before going to an exhibition outside of the Ethnological Museum in Berlin a detailed status report is written by the preservation department staff on every object which is part of the loan contract.

9 The "ILKAR"-project, a research project devoted to find "Integrated Solutions for Preservation, Archiving and Restoration of Endangered Magnetic Tapes and Cylinders" was running in Berlin for three years in cooperation with the Rathgen-Forschungslabor, National Museums in Berlin. See also the DVD ILKAR-Project

In general, the policy of the Berlin Phonogramm-Archiv is to digitise all wax cylinders and "to ensure sustained access to stored information" (Schüller 2005: 1) as in other sound archives.[10] However, most of these cylinders have been in use since the foundation of the archive more than a hundred years ago. In the course of time many cylinders have lost their primary quality: they have been damaged in various ways, and the stored information may not exist any more. It is therefore a special challenge to a sound archive to deal with cylinders like these. The ethical consequences go far beyond the usual tasks of an archive, because of the demand of preserving the unique historical sound, on the one hand, but, on the other, to consider the fragility of the object and the possible destruction of information. The archive's responsibility is to try all existing possibilities for the rescue and preservation of the sound, but there are no generally applicable concepts that would help the archivists to decide how to proceed. Considerations and guidelines as recommended, for example, by IASA (Bradley 2009), are helpful, but they are not applicable in all regards for the wax cylinder collection of the Berlin Phonogramm-Archiv. Therefore, it is always a personal decision of the archivists as to what should be preserved and what may be neglected.[11] "Since not everything can be saved, research archives have an obligation to preserve significant research-related materials [...] and their value must come from research use and community benefits" (Seeger 2010: 23).

IDENTIFICATION AND ARCHIVING

Identifying and archiving historical recordings requires information about the circumstances connected with a particular recording, the time and place of recording, information about the person who was recorded as well as information about the person who made the recording. The available data today are sometimes very poor, and only basic information can be found in

Documentation (*ILKAR* ... 2011).

10 Cf. also Koch and Ziegler 2009.

11 The discussion on ethics and rights is continuously prominent in archives and is not yet finished. See also Seeger 2010: 20.

the written sources. According to the questionnaire that was put together by the earlier director of the Berlin Museum für Völkerkunde Felix von Luschan and later enlarged by Erich von Hornbostel with a chapter on music, the collector was asked to obtain information about the ethnic group to which the performer belonged and his/her gender and age (Luschan 1904). Surprisingly, the names and background of the performers were obviously not important for researchers in the beginning of the 20th century.

Folk and traditional music were supposed to be common knowledge and anonymous, and supposedly no individual or personal style existed in folk or traditional music. Thus, for example, during World War I, the music of prisoners of war was recorded in Austrian and German prison camps, and these very few and more or less incidental recordings were taken as being representative for the entire music culture.[12] However, the prevailing assumption at that time, that every member of an ethnic group or society would possess the same musical knowledge and skills, proved to be wrong.

The same is also true for the collectors themselves. Although identified by name, there was little information about his or her background, education, preferences or interests either. It is, however, of significance that among the collectors of the Berlin wax cylinders, there were only a few persons, whose main profession was music. Namely, collections of European folk music arose from the efforts of enthusiasts, composers like Béla Bartók, Jón Leifs, Jenö von Takacs, or linguists and folklorists like Eduard Wolter, Matija Murko and others. The results are, of course, varied and different: If the collector was personally interested and devoted to music, he was able to judge the recordings and make a good choice in recording valuable material. However, if he was simply "doing his job"—as many of the missionaries, colonial officers, and ethnologists collecting for the archive outside of Europe—the collected material is probably not representative of the music cultures in the respective area.

Nevertheless, the information supplied by the collector himself must be treated as original, even if the present (political) situation does not corre-

12 Cf. for example Lachmann 1929, Nadel 1933, Schünemann 1923 and others.

spond with the historical data. The proper geographic identification is not only a problem when making an inventory of recordings made in Africa or Asia during colonial times, i.e. before 1918, but also for Europe, where especially in eastern and south-eastern regions borders and places changed rapidly throughout the whole 20th century.

For proper archival reference, information is also needed about the technical equipment that was used for a specific recording. This is very important, yet it was often neglected in former times. For example, the speed of recording wax cylinders was not announced. Since the phonograph allowed varying speed between 100 and 250 rpm, it was necessary to indicate the recording speed properly in order to enable correct replay. In the Berlin Phonogramm-Archiv the collector was asked to make an announcement at the start of the recording (what, where, when), and then blow the pitch pipe (435 Hz). Yet this important technical information is missing in about 40 % of all historical wax cylinder recordings.[13] If the music was not familiar to the technician or the person making an inventory of the data, serious mistakes could occur.

The situation is much easier in archives, where the collections do not go beyond the national or ethnic borders of a country and the holdings are generally more or less familiar to the archivist.

PRESERVATION

Preserving sound recordings means, first of all, the preservation of the physical integrity of the sound carrier as an object. Yet, equally important is the preservation of the information on the sound carrier, and it is impossible to separate object and information. According to IASA it is the archive's obligation to use "the best practices to ensure the physical and chemical integrity of the original documents" (Schüller 2005: 3).

Before digitising the first task is to provide the best possible physical status of the cylinder. In Berlin, besides the few original wax cylinders, new

13 Cf. also Wiedmann 2006.

Fig. 2: Damaged cylinders. Ethnologisches Museum, Staatliche Museen zu Berlin – Preußischer Kulturbesitz, 1994. Photo: Dietrich Graf.

positive copies from the galvano-negatives are used as the original carriers. The problem of providing new positive copies from the matrices has been solved. Thanks to the restoration and preservation departments in our institution, the wax cylinder collections are preserved in an acceptable physical state. However, the galvano-negatives, that is, the cylinder matrices, are of special interest, because so far no satisfactory solution for gaining the information directly from the galvanos has been found. These cylinders have to be stored and watched carefully, since there is a hope for a possible better playback in the future. Meanwhile, single galvanos have been digitised by applying new optical methods, but none of the different methods is applicable for the thousands of galvanos stored in the Berlin Phonogramm-Archiv.[14]

In Berlin we have tested several strategies to acquire the original sound, but we still follow the old-fashioned method of Hornbostel (Hornbostel 1923), which is simple, cheap and short. Playing wax cylinders on modern devices is no longer a problem. According to Albrecht Wiedmann, sound engineer at the Berlin Phonogramm-Archiv who has transferred more than 10,000 cylinders, the process of signal extraction from original carriers as described and discussed in IASA Guidelines (Bradley 2009: 31) is also applied in Berlin. In addition, he states that "initially the digitisation is done without any sound processing to obtain a digital 'master' file. A digital copy of this file can then be used and altered in any way for varying purposes without a loss of quality" (Wiedmann 2011: 62).

Problems occur when original cylinders—unique recordings—are seriously damaged and irreparably ruined. The decision about the extent to which cleaning and carrier restoration should be applied is always dependent upon the content. Preservation by all means is not the best option, and in order not to risk the health of the employees or the contamination of the collection in some cases the decision must be made against preservation. Figure 2 shows a box with damaged cylinders, which were destroyed by water during bad storage conditions in the 1960s in the German Democratic Republic (DDR). When the boxes were opened in 1991, it was not possible to take the cylinders out of their case and identify them, much less to think of gaining access to their contents. Should efforts be undertaken in order to retrieve the sound of these cylinders? Is there any hope that ruined cylinders like these can be handled some day in the future?

Should such heavily damaged cylinders be trapped in archives as dangerous and useless objects? It is beyond discussion that in such cases the information on the cylinder does not exist any more. So for what reason should these cylinders be preserved? Moreover, there are also cylinders that are not damaged at all or only slightly. However, when it comes to

14 For more information see Ziegler s.a.

playback, there is no signal and no sound audible; the information is completely lost. The reasons for this might be an extraordinary poor recording, continuous replay of the cylinder before galvanisation, or improper cleaning. Of course, we first look for a better copy; but if there is none available, what should we do with cylinders like these? Should they also be preserved? I would argue that one should decide against preservation and remove such objects as quickly as possible.

ACCESS

One of the most important tasks of an archive today is to make historical recordings available. Access should be provided to all interested persons, and it is one of our main obligations to return these recordings to those peoples or communities where they were once recorded. Even if the sound quality is not the best—and there might be also reasons to question the reliability of historical recordings, nevertheless, for the indigenous communities these recordings can provide the most valuable information about their past, and these communities can also provide substantial help in identifying and judging these (Seeger 2010).

Access will be provided to colleagues as well as to the interested public by means of personal visits to the Archive, correspondence, mass media and also by publishing and disseminating our holdings. Thereby, publication of historical sound recordings takes the many ethical, legal and commercial aspects into account, and this has already commenced. For example, successful cooperation between researchers in Australia, Papua New Guinea, Berlin and the Lihirian community in New Ireland has resulted in the publication of a CD that was funded by a local company and combines historical and contemporary recordings.[15] In the same way a CD with historical recordings, made on the island of Palau, Micronesia, in 1898–1899 and 1936 respectively, has been published in a cooperation between the Berlin Phonogramm-Archiv and The Bureau of Arts and Cultures of Palau, financially supported by UNESCO (Koch and Ziegler 2011a). Further, one of

15 CD "*Ae Tinil Wen Lir.*" *Music of Lihir.* LHR001. Lihir Gold Limited 2008.

the most recent CD-publications, "Eduard Wolter's cylinders recorded in Lithuania, held in the Berlin Phonogramm-Archiv (1908–1909)," is the result of cooperation between the Institute of Lithuanian Literature and Folklore in Vilnius and the Berlin Phonogramm-Archiv (Nakienė and Žarskienė 2011). In all of these cases there was close cooperation between the Berlin Phonogramm-Archiv and the communities from where the historical recordings stem. However, in the case of the Palauan recordings, the texts have not been identified until now. On the contrary, the texts and musical notes of the Lithuanian recordings are published in the booklet and —according to the Lithuanian editors—serve as most valuable examples for folk music revival in Lithuania.

The Archive receives many requests from researchers and also communities or even private persons, who are interested in the music recorded in former times. But before providing access to everyone, we must ensure that there is real scientific or even national interest, and not simply commercial interests. Research and dissemination are closely linked, because in the case of historical recordings dissemination without prior research is not possible. There is no sense in publishing or disseminating historical recordings without providing background information.

PUBLICATION

The main intention of our Archive is to publish the holdings in an appropriate manner. Several publications are already on the market.[16] A comprehensive wax cylinder catalogue, which includes a book and a CD-ROM, was published in 2006 (Ziegler 2006). It provides detailed access to the collections by means of the combination of an introductory and explanatory text, a catalogue, documentation, sound examples and a compilation of the biographies of the individual collectors as well as indices and a bibliography. Within the CD-series *Berliner Phonogramm-Archiv – Historical Sound Recordings* the publication of the wax cylinders according to

16 The complete catalogue is to be found at www.smb.museum.

specific topics, collectors or geographic areas started in 2003. Meanwhile seven CDs are already on the market, and others are in preparation.

A publication includes a CD with sound recordings as well as a comprehensive booklet. In contrast to the digital 1 : 1 copies, which are preserved in the Berlin Phonogramm-Archiv without any changes, the sound examples on the CDs were slightly cleaned for publication. The accompanying booklet is in two languages and includes photographs and musical notes (transcriptions); moreover, it offers insight into the historical, ethnographical and ethnomusicological background of the respective recordings as well as the collector. The CDs are always produced in close contact with specialists for the respective region; they are responsible for the selection of recordings to be published and for the text. In any case, joint research and joint publication projects are our first concern.

The publication policy in Berlin is different from the publication of historical recordings in the Vienna Phonogrammarchiv. Vienna decided to publish their historical recordings in a tripartite arrangement of the edition, sound recordings on audio CDs, original protocols and files on a data CD and printed commentaries in the CD booklet (Schüller 1999). In Berlin, on the contrary, only a selection of the recordings is published. This is mainly due to the specific sound carrier, since the recordings on wax plates in Vienna, which have been recorded with the Vienna Archiv-Phonograph possess a better quality than the wax cylinders in Berlin. In addition, in our CD publications the original documentation is not added as data files as in Vienna, but is included in the commentaries.

The following example clearly reveals the difficulties in publishing historical wax cylinder recordings. CDs 4 and 5 of our CD series present unique recordings of indigenous Indian music (*música aborigen*) and popular music (*música criolla*), which were made in Argentina between 1905 and 1909 by the German scholar Robert Lehmann-Nitsche (1872–1938) (Koch and Ziegler 2009). There was a lively discussion about whether the unique and only existing recording of the musical bow *kolo* recorded in 1905 should be included in the publication or not. This example has been discussed at length, since different kinds of source and research materials are avail-

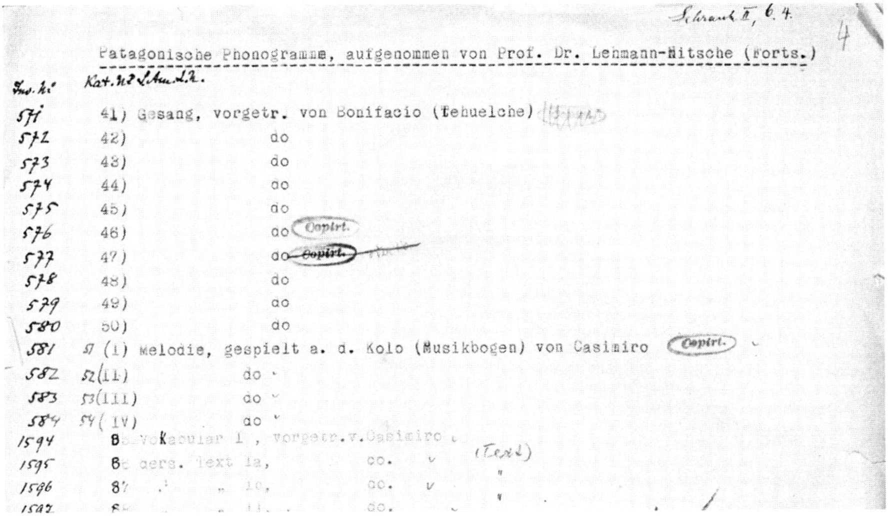
Schrank II, 6. 4.

Patagonische Phonogramme, aufgenommen von Prof. Dr. Lehmann-Nitsche (Forts.)

Inv. Nr. Kat. Nr. Lehm. N.

571 41) Gesang, vorgetr. von Bonifacio (Tehuelche)
572 42) do
573 43) do
574 44) do
575 45) do
576 46) do Copirt.
577 47) do Copirt.
578 48) do
579 49) do
580 50) do
581 51 (I) Melodie, gespielt a. d. Kolo (Musikbogen) von Casimiro Copirt.
582 52(II) do
583 53(III) do
584 54(IV) do
1594 8. Vokabular I, vorgetr.v.Casimiro
1595 8. ders. Text Ia, do. (Text)
1596 8. „ „ Ib, do.
1597 8. „ „ II, do.

Fig. 3: Documentation of the collection "Patagonien," recorded by Robert Lehmann-Nitsche in La Plata, Argentina in 1905. Berlin Phonogramm-Archiv. Ethnologisches Museum, Staatliche Museen zu Berlin – Preußischer Kulturbesitz.

Fig. 4: Tehuelche singer Casimiro, playing the musical bow kolo. *La Plata, 1905. Ethnologisches Museum, Staatliche Museen zu Berlin – Preußischer Kulturbesitz. Photo: Robert Lehmann-Nitsche.*

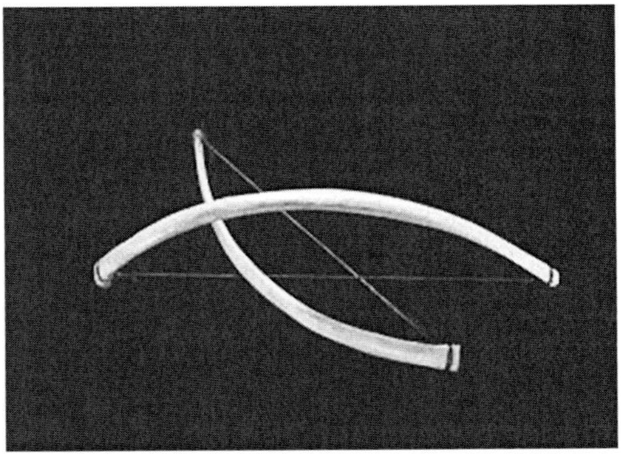

Fig. 5: Two musical bows kolo *from the collection of Robert Lehmann-Nitsche. Inv. Nr: V c 8529a + b. Ethnologisches Museum, Staatliche Museen zu Berlin – Preußischer Kulturbesitz, 2007. Photo: Martin Franken.*

Fig. 6: Transcription by Erich Fischer of wax cyl. 51 kolo *(Fischer 1908: 961).*

able: the wax cylinder and the documentation list of Lehmann-Nitsche (Fig. 3), a photo of the player of the musical bow (Fig. 4), the instrument itself in the museum collection (Fig. 5), and in addition articles written by the collector on "Patagonian songs and the musical bow" (Lehmann-Nitsche 1908) and by Erich Fischer, including transcriptions of texts and music (Fischer 1908), among them also a transcription of the music played on the musical bow (Fig. 6). Thus, the importance of this example is obvious, but the recording quality is extremely poor and cannot be improved. We nevertheless decided to include this recording on CD in order to demonstrate its historical value.

CONCLUSION

Wax cylinder recordings form a special genre among the holdings of ethnomusicological archives; they are unique historical sources, but also cause different kinds of problems. For purely answering technical questions, the IASA and other associations and institutions provides useful information; yet, as far as the content is concerned, the archives have to decide themselves what to do with these historical recordings. Without background information, however, these recordings would be trapped in the archive, and at the same time trapped in history; they cannot be used for ethnomusicological research and would serve for acoustical purposes only. As archivists working in sound archives, we therefore have to ask ourselves whether it makes any sense to publish historical recordings lacking information, or, better, let them slumber in the archives until someone draws them out of oblivion. If the archive decides to preserve them, technical knowledge and proper storage conditions are needed, but these are of course dependent upon the financial possibilities of the respective institution.

Historical recordings need special treatment, not only because of their fragile and sensitive physical material, but also because of their unique content. If we cannot gain information from historical examples of music cultures, which were recorded long ago and far away, they cannot be regarded as useful "ethnomusicological" sources. The daily work in the Berlin Phonogramm-Archiv has often proven that the historical value of unique wax cylinder recordings does not correspond with their sound quality. Instead, the older the historical recordings are, the more their value increases. Seeger (2010: 16) mentions "the long tale of the use of archival recordings," but only few wax cylinders have a fairly good sound quality, which is partly due to the recording skills of the collector, but also due to good preservation and storage conditions. Colleagues are often quite enthusiastic about specific wax cylinder recordings when reading the documentation, but they are very disappointed when they finally listen to the sound. Digitisation and preservation are necessary, but not in every case. Sound cleaning and reconstruction are possible to a certain extent, but if the original sound is not reversible and lost forever and access therefore not possible, I would argue that the archive should be free to decide to dispose of it. There is no reason to preserve trapped material in the archive, which is out of use and causes only problems and expenses.

Time goes by, and therefore, I would like to remind all colleagues to take more notice of historical sources in ethnomusicological archives before the insiders' knowledge about the historical recordings is completely forgotten and the unique historical recordings confined in the archives could only serve as useless remains of the past.

REFERENCES

Bradley, Kevin (ed.)
2009 *Guidelines on the production and preservation of digital audio objects (IASA Technical Committee – Standards, Recommended Practices and Strategies, IASA-TC 04),* second edition. Canberra: International Association of Sound and Audiovisual Archives (IASA).

Fischer, Erich
1908 Patagonische Musik. *Anthropos* 3: 941–961.

Gütl, Clemens et al. (eds.)
2010 *Jahrbuch 1 des Phonogrammarchivs der Österreichischen Akademie der Wissenschaften. Beiträge des internationalen Symposiums 110 Jahre Phonogrammarchiv: Reflexionen über Arbeitsfelder, Kooperationen und Perspektiven.* Göttingen: Cuvillier Verlag.

Hornbostel, Erich Moritz von
1923 Phonographische Methoden. In: Abdelhalden, Emil (ed.), *Handbuch der biologischen Arbeitsmethoden, Abt. V, Teil 7.* Berlin: Urban and Schwarzenberg, 419–438.

ILKAR ...
2011 *ILKAR-Project Documentation. Integrierte Lösungen zur Konservierung, Archivierung und Restaurierung gefährdeter Magnetbänder und Walzen. / Integrated Solutions for Preservation, Archiving and Restoration of Endangered Magnetic Tapes and Cylinders.* Berlin: Staatliche Museen zu Berlin – Kulturstiftung des Bundes, Kulturstiftung der Länder. (DVD-ROM)

Koch, Lars-Christian, and Susanne Ziegler (eds.)
2009 *Robert Lehmann-Nitsche – Walzenaufnahmen aus Argentinien 1905–1909. Grabaciones en cilindros de Argentina.* BPhA–WA 4/5. Berlin: Staatliche Museen zu Berlin – Stiftung Preußischer Kulturbesitz. (CD)

2011 *Walzenaufnahmen aus Palau, Mikronesien / Wax Cylinder Recordings from Palau, Micronesia / Chesols er a Belau, Micronesia el Mlengai el Ousbech a "Wax Cylinder" 1909–1936.* BPhA–WA 6. Berlin: Staatliche Museen zu Berlin – Stiftung Preußischer Kulturbesitz. (CD)

Koch, Lars-Christian, et al.
2009 ILKAR: Integrated Solutions for Preservation, Archiving and Conservation of Endangered Magnetic Tapes and Cylinders. *IASA Journal* 33: 41–49.

Lachmann, Robert
1929 *Musik des Orients.* Breslau: Ferdinand Hirt.

Lehmann-Nitsche, Robert
1908 Patagonische Gesänge und Musikbogen. *Anthropos* 3: 916–940.

Luschan, Felix von
1904 *Anleitung für ethnographische Beobachtungen und Sammlungen in Afrika und Ozeanien.* 3rd ed. L. Musik. Berlin: Königl. Museum für Völkerkunde in Berlin.

Nadel, Siegfried
1933 *Georgische Gesänge.* Berlin/Lautabteilung. Leipzig: Kommissionsverlag Otto Harrassowitz.

Nakienė, Austė, and Rūta Žarskienė (eds.)
2011 *Eduardo Volterio Lietuvoje Įrašyti Voleliai (1908–1909), Saugomi Berlyno Fonogramų Archyve / Eduard Wolter's Cylinders Recorded in Lithuania (1908–1909), held in the Berlin Phonogramm-Archiv.* Vilnis: Institute of Lithuanian Literature and Folklore. (CD)

Schüller, Dietrich
1999 General editor's preface. *Tondokumente aus dem Phonogrammarchiv der Österreichischen Akademie der Wissenschaften. Gesamtausgabe der Historischen Bestände 1899-1950. Series 1: The First Expeditions 1901 to Croatia, Brazil, and the Isle of Lesbos.* Wien: Verlag der Österreichischen Akademie der Wissenschaften. (CD)

2005 (ed.) *The Safeguarding of the Audio Heritage: Ethics, Principles and Preservation Strategy. (IASA Technical Committee - Standards, Recommended Practices and Strategies, IASA–TC 03), Version 3.* International Association of Sound and Audiovisual Archives (IASA).

Schünemann, Georg
1923 *Das Lied der deutschen Kolonisten in Rußland. (Sammelbände für Vergleichende Musikwissenschaft, 3. Band).* München: Drei Masken Verlag.

Seeger, Anthony
2010 Looking to the Past and Creating the Future: The Function and Ethics of Audiovisual Archives in the 21st Century. In: Gütl, Clemens et al. (eds.), *Jahrbuch 1 des Phonogrammarchivs der Österreichischen Akademie der Wissenschaften. Beiträge des internationalen Symposiums 110 Jahre Phonogrammarchiv: Reflexionen über Arbeitsfelder, Kooperationen und Perspektiven.* Göttingen: Cuvillier Verlag, 13–29.

Seeger, Anthony, and Shubha Chaudhuri (eds.)
2004 *Archives for the Future – Global Perspectives on Audiovisual Archives in the 21st Century.* Gurgaon, Haryana, India: Archives and Research Centre for Ethnomusicology, American Institute of Indian Studies; Calcutta: Seagull Books.

Simon, Artur (ed.)
2000 *Das Berliner Phonogrammarchiv 1900–2000. Sammlungen der traditionellen Musik der Welt. = The Berlin Phonogramm-Archiv 1900–2000. Collections of Traditional Music of the World.* Berlin: VWB – Verlag für Wissenschaft und Bildung.

Simon, Artur, and Ulrich Wegner (eds.)
2000 *Music! 100 Recordings. 100 Years of the Berlin Phonogramm-Archiv 1900–2000.* Berlin: Museum Collection Berlin – Schott Wergo. (CDs)

Wiedmann, Albrecht

2000 Einige technische Bemerkungen zur digitalen Konservierung der alten Bestände des Berliner Phonogramm-Archivs. In: Simon, Artur (ed.), *Das Berliner Phonogramm-Archiv 1900–2000. Sammlungen der traditionellen Musik der Welt.* Berlin: VWB – Verlag für Wissenschaft und Bildung, 203–208.

2006 Restaurierung und Digitalisierung der Bestände des Berliner Phonogramm-Archivs. In: Ziegler, Susanne, *Die Wachszylinder des Berliner Phonogramm-Archivs.* Berlin: Ethnologisches Museum, Staatliche Museen zu Berlin – Preußischer Kulturbesitz, 35–38.

2011 Transferring and Editing of the Wax Cylinders. In: Koch, Lars-Christian, and Susanne Ziegler (eds.), *Walzenaufnahmen aus Südosteuropa / Wax Cylinder Recordings from Southeast Europe: G. Küppers-Sonnenberg* 1935–39. BPhA–WA 7. Berlin: Staatliche Museen zu Berlin – Stiftung Preußischer Kulturbesitz. (CD)

Ziegler, Susanne

2006 *Die Wachszylinder des Berliner Phonogramm-Archivs.* Berlin: Ethnologisches Museum, Staatliche Museen zu Berlin – Preußischer Kulturbesitz.

s.a. The Berlin Phonogramm-Archiv and its Activities in Preserving the Musical Cultures of the World. In: Simon, Stefan et al. (ed.), *Proceedings of the Symposium "Public-Private Partnership in the Management of Cultural Heritage Assets – a European Challenge", Berlin, 15./16.5. 2007.* (Manuscript, submitted for publication).

CONTRIBUTORS

Alma Bejtullahu, MA, finished her undergraduate studies in musicology and graduate studies in ethnomusicology at the University of Ljubljana. She is a PhD candidate at Institutum Studiorum Humanitatis Graduate School of the Humanities in Ljubljana. Most of her research work includes issues like gender, modernity and tradition, music and politics, music and war either in Kosovo or in Slovenia. She is the author of several papers that analyze the transgression of female musicians in Kosovo to the public area, female polka musicians in Slovenia and musical practices of Albanian catholic communities in different geographical areas.

E-mail: almabejtullahu@yahoo.com

Nick Green, MA (Dance) independant researcher, has been teaching and researching traditional dance in Southeastern Europe for over 25 years whilst working as a professional chartered engineer. He recently completed a part-time MA at De Montfort University, Leicester, studying dance practices in Timişoara and is a member of the ICTM Study Group on Music and Dance in Southeastern Europe, and the ICTM Study Group on Ethnochoreology.

E-mail: eliznik@eliznik.org.uk, eliznik@hotmail.com

Katalin Juhász, PhD, is an ethnographer and senior research fellow at the Institute of Ethnology, Research Center for Humanities, Hungarian Academy of Sciences in Budapest (Hungary). Her main topic of research is personal hygiene, concept of cleanliness, ritual washing. As a folk singer, and an active participant in the Hungarian dance house movement she is interested in questions of preserving, recreation, and renewal of folk traditions.

E-mail: drjuhaszkatica@gmail.com

Drago Kunej, PhD, is the head of the Sound Archives at the Institute of Ethnomusicology ZRC SAZU and an assistant professor at the Academy of Music and at the Faculty of Arts. He received a degree in Electrical Engineering and his master's and PhD degree in musical acoustics from the University of Ljubljana (Slovenia). His research is focused on the technical and methodological aspects of documentary ethnomusicological field sound recordings and early sound recordings in Slovenia. He is actively involved in the problems of sound preservation, restoration, re-recording, digitisation, and archiving.

E-mail: drago.kunej@zrc-sazu.si

Rebeka Kunej, PhD, is an ethnochoreologist and a research fellow at the Institute of Ethnomusicology ZRC SAZU. She has a BA in ethnology and cultural antropology and a MA and PhD in folklore studies. Her interests include dance and dancing in Slovenia, especially in connection with Slovenian folk dance, its transformations, and the impact folklorism has on it. Her recent research has been dedicated to contemporary dance events as the components of large-scale events, and to old 78 rpm gramophone records as an important source of folkloristic research.

E-mail: rebeka.kunej@zrc-sazu.si

Zlata Marjanović, MPhil, finished her undergraduate study in ethnomusicology at the Faculty of Music, Department for Musicology and Ethnomusicology in Belgrade (Serbia). Since 2005, she has worked as a lecturer of ethnomusicology, traditional singing and traditional playing in the "Mokranjac" High music school in Kraljevo. Her research is focused mainly on the musical traditions of the Montenegrin Coast and Hinterland.

E-mail: aurelliakramberger@gmail.com

Liz Mellish, MA, is a part time PhD student at UCL – School of Slavonic and East European Studies. She has been teaching and researching traditional dance in Southeastern Europe for around 25 years. Following her return to academic studies in 2003 she completed a MA in Central and South East European Studies, and is currently writing up her PhD on the lives of Romanian folk dancers in the city of Timişoara. She is secretary of the ICTM Study Group on Music and Dance in Southeastern Europe, and a member of the ICTM Study Group on Ethnochoreology.

E-mail: eliznik@eliznik.org.uk, liz.mellish@ucl.ac.uk

Selena Rakočević, PhD, gained her doctorate *Dance and dance music of the Banat Serbs in the light of their mutual relationships* in 2009 at the University of Arts, Belgrade. Her fields of professional interests are the musical and dance tradition of Vojvodina in the light of the multicultural and multiethnic context; ethnochoreology; music/dance relationships; contemporary music and dance. Selena Rakočević is an assistant professor at the Department of Ethnomusicology, Faculty of Music, Belgrade, as well at the Academy of Arts, Novi Sad. She teaches ethnochoreology at both faculties.

E-mail: selena@rakocevic.rs

Zoltán Szabó, MA, is an ethnographic specialist, head of Applied Folk Arts Section of the Hungarian Heritage House (Budapest) and bagpipe teacher at Hungarian Folk Music School in Óbuda (Budapest). He started playing the bagpipe in 1979 and performs from authentic folk to jazz music. As a curator of the County Museum in Pécs (1985–1992), then the Museum of Ethnography in Budapest (1992–2007), his main themes were peasant farming, traditional fishing and crafts. During these years he became acquainted with all types of bagpipe used in the Carpathian Basin and the Balkans, as a musician and as an ethnographer museologist.

E-mail: abaiszabozoltan@gmail.com

Urša Šivic, PhD, finished her undergraduate, graduate and PhD studies in musicology at the University of Ljubljana (Slovenia). She is employed as a researcher in ethnomusicology at the Institute of Ethnomusicology ZRC SAZU in Ljubljana. She is involved in field work collecting vocal material with the focus on the analysis of elements of Slovenian ways of singing, on its specific factors that influence the ways of its changing. Her research work also includes adaptations of "foreign" musics in the Slovenian cultural area, customs related to music and transformations of folk music in popular music.

E-mail: ursa@zrc-sazu.si

David Verbuč, MPhil, is a PhD candidate in ethnomusicology at UC Davis, USA. He worked (and occasionally still works) as a music journalist for various Slovenian media. In 2008, he issued a double CD of his own field recordings of folk songs from the Upper Savinja Valley in North Slovenia. Verbuč is currently conducting his dissertation fieldwork research on house concert scenes in the US, and the relations between place/space, music, and social practices.

E-mail: dverbuc@ucdavis.edu

Susanne Ziegler, PhD, graduated in Musicology/Ethnomusicology and Slavic languages and literature at the University of Cologne. Since 1993 she has held a position in the Berlin Phonogramm-Archiv at the Ethnomusicology department of the Ethnological Museum, National Museums in Berlin. She has published numerous scientific articles on the Berlin Phonogramm-Archiv as well as on music in Southeastern Europe, Turkey, and the Caucasus. She is chair of the ICTM Study Group on Historical Sources of Traditional Music.

E-mail: s.ziegler@smb.spk-berlin.de